Mysterious Oklahoma

Eerie True Tales From The Sooner State

Mysterious Oklahoma

Eerie True Tales From The Sooner State

David A. Farris

LITTLE BRUCE
Edmond, Oklahoma

Mysterious Oklahoma
Eerie True Tales From The Sooner State

Written by David A. Farris

Edited by Judith A. Tillinghast, Ph.D.

Illustrations by Suzanne King Randall

Book Production, Michael S. Carter, M.S. Graphics

Copyright ©1995 by David A. Farris
Published by Little Bruce
P.O. Box 5991 • Edmond, Oklahoma 73083-5991

All rights reserved. No part of this work may be reproduced or transmitted in any form by any means without the written permission of the publisher.

ISBN 0-9646922-0-1

Printed in the United States of America

For my parents.

Acknowledgments

Sandra Merrick for helping me get started with my research.

Judy A. Tillinghast, Ph.D. for all her help with this book.

Steve Wagner and Paul Moore from the
Oklahoma Department of Wildlife Conservation
for supplying me with research materials and photos.

Richard Seifried, Jean Waller Seifried and all the good folks of the
Oklahoma Mutual UFO Network for pictures and information.

The good folks at the Oklahoma Historical Society
for helping me find photographs.

Special thanks go to the following for
allowing me the use of their material:
Randy Renner of KWTV Channel 9
Faber and Faber, Inc.
Loren Coleman
Hayden C. Hewes
The Daily Oklahoman
Fate Magazine

Contents

Introduction..xi
Welcome To My World

Chapter 1 17
Ancient Okies and Prehistoric Tourists

Chapter 2..25
The Spirits of Oklahoma

Chapter 3..33
Strange Sooner Skies

Chapter 4..40
Close Encounters Over Ottawa

Chapter 5..45
The Mysterious Sooner State Spook Lights

Chapter 6..49
Crop Circles and Landing Sites in the "Wavin' Wheat"

Chapter 7..55
Oklahomans and Alien Abductions

Chapter 8..65
Mysterious Mutilators

Chapter 9..79
Mysterious Cats and Other Strange Four-Legged Creatures

Chapter 10..**87**
Bigfoot, Wild Monkeys and Other Strange, Hairy Bipeds in the Sooner State

Chapter 11 ....**101**
"You Should Have Seen The One That Got Away"

Chapter 12 ....**107**
A Potpourri of Sooner State Strangeness

Map of Oklahoma's 'Spooky Spots' **113**

References **115**

The Journey Begins...

"The most beautiful thing we can experience is the mysterious. It is the source of all true art and science."
– Albert Einstein

Introduction: Welcome To My World

Ever since I was a child I've loved spooky tales. It was during my grade school years when I first heard tales of ghosts and UFOs, told by classmates who swore the stories to be true. I believe, when we're quite young, most children become familiar with the more popular urban legends such as the "disappearing hitch-hiker" and "the bloody hook found hanging on the car door." Because we were children, we turned to our parents and teachers and asked, "Are these stories really true?" "No," they would usually reply, and that would resolve the issue, at least until someone else came up with another story.

Towards the fourth and fifth grades we could order books as a class from a mail order book store. Included in the selection were books, marketed as nonfiction, dealing with subjects such as ghosts, UFOs, psychic phenomena, and Bigfoot. This was during the 70's, when information concerning such topics became more mainstream. America learned the name Erich von Daniken, who explained his theory of ancient extraterrestrial architects in his 1968 book, *Chariots of the Gods?* In 1973, whether it was real or just mass hysteria, an intense period of UFO activity was being reported worldwide. Then came the classic book and movie *The Exorcist*, which depicted "demonic possession." An environment, open minded to the existence of such strange things, was being created. UFOs and Bigfoot documentaries were quite popular at this time and could be seen at movie theaters and on TV. Names such as Betty and Barney Hill, Travis Walton (p. 57) and Sasquatch (p. 87) became well known. At this point, reassurances from adults who claimed these stories were untrue seemed insincere. Thus began a lifelong fascination with unexplained phenomena.

After graduating from college I was in need of some "escapism." I found refuge at the local public library. It had been years since I had gone to the library to look up something for fun, instead of getting information for a class or studying for a test. I found myself in the nonfiction section, amazed at the large selection of books dealing with such subjects as UFOs, ghosts, psychic phenomena, strange beasts and other such anomalies too numerous to list. As I began my journey through this maze of unusual information, I learned there is a name for people who engage in such a pastime. The terms "fortean" (a person who studies such strange, unexplained phenomena) and "forteana" (the strange, unexplained phenomena being studied) were coined in honor of the man Charles Hoy Fort. Because of his influence, no book of forteana would be complete without introducing the reader to Mr. Fort.

Charles Hoy Fort was born in Albany, New York in 1874. Not much is known about his early life, except that he studied journalism and zoology. After coming into a modest but adequate inheritance he was able to pursue any interest of his choice, which was researching the strange and unknown. Most of his research took place at the New York Public Library and the British Museum in London. Fort would gather tales of the strange and bizarre from vast collections of journals and newspapers. The staggering amount of information he found has been chronicled in four books: *The Book of the Damned, Lo!, New Lands,* and *Wild Talents.* To honor the man who fascinated so many people, associations like the International Fortean Organization and the journal, *Fortean Times,* were inspired. Charles Fort died in 1932. Although the original Fortean Society was established in the 1920's (during his lifetime) by such intellectuals as Clarence Darrow and Oliver Wendell Homes, Fort refused membership.

I was fascinated by forteana long before I was aware of the term. I have spent hours sorting through strange tales. Some were obvious hoaxes or fairy tales, however some were well documented, first-hand reports from credible witnesses. Every now and again, I would come across a story from Oklahoma. Eventually, I became inspired to seek out specifically, strange tales from the Sooner State. It wasn't long before I had a notebook full of stories encompassing a wide range of paranormal events. I learned "the wilds" of Oklahoma are rich with tales of strange beasts and the lakes and rivers alive with rumors of overgrown fish that could attack a man! These stories brought a rich, romantic color to my native state, as well as making any outdoor expedition more exciting. If the land or water beasts didn't get you, a UFO still could! It may sound silly, a full grown adult getting so excited over strange tales that very well may just be legend, but that's probably because you're reading these tales in the security of a civilization, complete with 911. If you were contemplating such eerie tales while, say, camped out in the deep woods of McCurtain County, the information contained in this book wouldn't seem so far fetched, especially around midnight while listening to the wind blowing through the trees. I'd bet even the bravest of us would be listening very closely, hoping everything we hear is "just the wind."

   I didn't write this book in an attempt to prove anything or change anyone's mind about the world. My point is, a world without mystery would be very boring. There would be nothing but the cold harsh reality of the (so called) "real world." It seems to me, the closer one comes to a mystery, the more real it becomes. This is why I enjoy mysterious tales from my home state. I'm more familiar with the location of the events and, if so moved, may travel there with relatively little effort. I have enjoyed these homespun tales for years and hope the readers of my work will enjoy them every bit as much. Please bear in mind, when I say "true stories," I mean stories that have been told as true, as opposed to stories told as myth or legend. I realize a story is only as credible as its source, and admittedly, some tales will seem more credible than others. I am merely providing the stories (as well as the sources) as I found them, leaving the reader free to draw a conclusion all their own. Personally, true or not, the feeling of awe and wonder they inspire is real enough for me.

David A. Farris

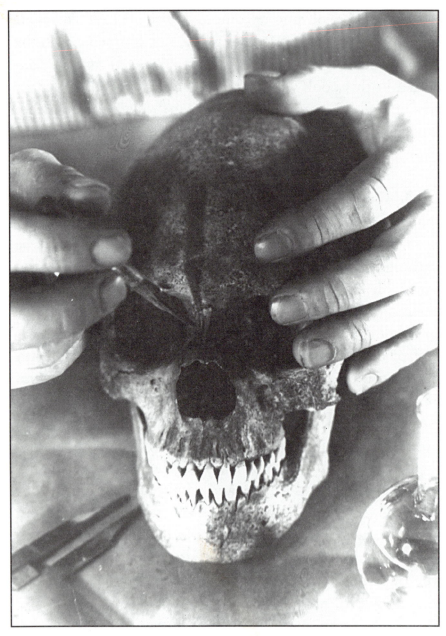

Working on a skull from Spiro Mounds at a laboratory.

Photo Courtesy of the Archives & Manuscripts Division of the Oklahoma Historical Society

1 Ancient Okies And Prehistoric Tourists

Written historical records of the area now known as Oklahoma only go back as far as 1541. Until 1541, the past was interpreted by archaeologists and anthropologists who studied ancient ruins. Then, as now, anyone migrating across the continent would most likely pass through the panhandle state.

Prehistoric Oklahoma was ideal for nomadic tribes of big-game hunters. The weather was moderate, and natural shelters like caves and projecting rock ledges were abundant. This could explain why Oklahoma is one of the oldest areas in the United States in terms of human occupation.

The oldest prehistoric human discovery in Oklahoma is the Domebo mammoth kill-site uncovered near Stecker. It was named for the large number of mammoth skeletons excavated from the area. Carbon-14 tests date the material found at the site as between 10,243 to 11,061 years of age. The spear tips found within the rib cages of the skeletons were determined to be the products of Clovis man; Oklahoma's oldest discovered family. The wandering hunters traveled the same routes season after season, following herds of big game. The largest quarry hunted was the Columbian mammoth. Oklahoma was a maze of jungle and swamps, the preferred climate of the Columbian mammoth and other creatures hunted for food and hides. The hunters camped by creeks and river banks during the warmer months, retreating to the shelter of the rock ledges and caves as the weather turned colder. The caves of the panhandle, the caves and ledges of the Ozarks, and scattered creeks and riverbed sites yielded signs of prehistoric human existence.

A few promising areas of interest to amateur archaeologists are; Fourche Maline Creek near its junction with the Poteau River (southeast Oklahoma), the caves near Kenton (panhandle), the Cedar Creek Site (Caddo County), and the Williams Mound (about two miles from the junction of Furche Maline Creek with the Poteau River).

The Spiro epoch (500 A.D. to 1300 A.D.) marked an important period of Oklahoma prehistory. The remains of the Spiro Mounds are easy to find (Spiro Oklahoma, between Sallisaw and Poteau); and constitute Oklahoma's only archaeological park. The 140-acre site includes 12 southern mounds containing the remains of an Indian culture that lived at the site from 850 A.D. to 1450 A.D. Considered one of the four most important prehistoric Indian sites east of the Rocky Mountains, the Spiro Mounds are believed to be part of the "Southern Cult," an association of mound sites built and used during the Mississippian Period.

Early explorers also left their mark in Oklahoma. Many clues have been found suggesting a variety of cultures may have explored the state in prehistoric times. The Arkansas, Canadian and Cimarron Rivers bear the signs of ancient explorers who sailed through the state. The oldest discovered runestone carving is the Pontotoc Stone in Pontotoc County dated 500 B.C.

Symbols belonging to many different cultures have been found, but who actually carved them is unknown. The best example of this would be the runestones found in and around the town of Heavener. The most famous site of such carvings is found in Runestone State Park, in Heavener. From all indications it appears that vikings sailed up the Arkansas River 480 years before Columbus first arrived in America. The main attraction is a huge rock, twelve feet high and ten feet wide, marked with eight rune characters. First discovered by relocated Choctaws, in 1828, it was later named Indian Rock in 1898, when it was discovered by white settlers. As more settlers arrived in the area, more runestones were discovered. The residents around Heavener learned to look carefully when encountering a rock ledge or other possible runestone hiding places. Other suspected runestones were found, but none as spectacular as the huge slab of granite at Heavener. Scores of authorities from different fields of expertise attempted to translate the inscriptions. The symbols are thought to be from two separate runic alphabets, and dating from two different periods of time. The symbols were transliterated to Latin letters and were believed by some to read GNOMEDAL. A literal translation of the message would be Sun Dial Valley or Valley of the Boundary Marker.

In 1967, a couple of men from California took on the task of deciphering the message, once and for all. Two men, O.G. Landsverk, a Norse specialist, and Alf Monge, a retired United States Army cryptographer, shook Oklahoma history by declaring the runestones were not messages, but dates. The men read the cryptogram at Heavener eight different

Heavener's Rune Stone.

Photo Courtesy of the Archives & Manuscripts Division of the Oklahoma Historical Society

ways before confirming the date November 11, 1012, A.D. Other, lesser runestones were also confirmed as dates, the oldest being November 24, 1024, A.D., which can be seen at the Kerr Museum near Poteau. Similar runestones have been discovered as far east as Arkansas and as far west as the Texas Panhandle. Some skeptics believe other cultures besides the vikings are responsible for the carvings, while others believe the whole thing a hoax. All I can suggest is that you go to Heavener and see for yourself. At the very least, you're guaranteed an awe inspiring experience in some of Oklahoma's most beautiful country.

Signs of ancient unknown cultures have been found in highly populated areas. In June 1969 a construction crew was building a grocery warehouse in the area of 122nd and Broadway Extension, just south of Edmond. Workmen unearthed what appeared to be the foundation of an ancient structure. The stones were set along perfect, parallel lines, pointing east, forming a diamond shape. No clues have been found to indicate which culture built the foundation. According to Durwood Pate, an Oklahoma City geologist who studied the site, "We found post holes which measure a perfect rod apart, and a third portion of the stone surface measures almost a perfect two rods from the other two." He then concluded, "Everything is too well placed to be a natural formation."

During the time of the find, geologist Delbert Smith was president of Oklahoma Seismograph Company. He agreed with Pate when he declared, "There is no question about it. It has been laid there, but I have no idea by whom."

The site was discovered under 33 inches of top soil. No

items were found that could be tested for carbon-14, so its age, just like its builders, is undetermined.

"The Mayan Indians of Central America used stone floors," Pate told the Edmond Booster.

"The Plains Indians didn't use stone floors, but it is possible they could have," he added.

Not everyone who studied the site agreed it was carved by an ancient culture. Dr. Robert Bell, a professor of anthropology from Oklahoma University, visited the site in hope of finding Indian ruins. After examining the site, he determined it was a natural formation of sandstone and lime. The doctor said he had seen the same type of formation in the past.

Workers who uncovered the site estimated it to be about thirty-six yards, however Smith said it appeared to cover several thousand square feet. The latter estimate would seem more consistent with the natural formation opinion. Regardless of who was right, the warehouse was built, and the issue was laid to rest, unresolved.

In a real stretch of the imagination, evidence exists that may suggest Chinese explorers visited ancient Oklahoma approximately 2000 years before the birth of Christ. It was some time during the late 1940's when A.E. Eckert and his wife were digging a well north of Luther. A stick of dynamite blew free an odd looking chunk of red clay. Mrs. Eckert washed away the object's encasing to find a Chinese statuette. The Eckerts brought their find to the Benedictine Convent, then located in Guthrie. Sister Mary Placida showed the statuette to some native Chinese students who identified the old man, carrying a lamb and a staff, as Shu

Shing Lao, Chinese god of longevity. Experts at the University of Chicago determined the figure was carved from a species of tree that had been extinct for hundreds of years. A clue to its origin may have been found in the *Mountain Sea Classic*, a compilation of books recording ancient Chinese events beginning around 1440 B.C.

According to Henriette Mertz, in her book *Pale Ink*, the *Mountain Sea Classic* indicates two Chinese expeditions to America; one in the 5th century A.D., and an earlier one in the 23rd century B.C. The story indicates the explorers landed in the area of Mexico. Their accounts of the ancient culture were later confirmed by archaeologists. Is it possible these ancient explorers could have traveled as far north as Oklahoma? The most accepted explanation is that the statuette was stolen, finding its way to the state via outlaws.

In the late 1890's, bandits who robbed the Wells Fargo Bank in San Francisco made their way to Oklahoma. The outlaws camped along the old Ozark Trail, just north of Luther. It was there they hid their loot before being either killed or captured by lawmen. During this period in American history, San Francisco had a large Chinese population. Although a number of coincidences exist, no one knows for sure.

I believe, if the statuette found north of Luther wasn't part of the hidden Wells Fargo loot, it had to be someone else's hidden loot. Oklahoma was a notorious hide out for outlaws during the 1800's. One can only guess how many outlaws stashed their loot while hiding out in Oklahoma, only to be killed or sent to prison where they died. It seems likely that unretrieved treasure is still hiding in remote, undeveloped areas of the state.

Oklahoma has a rich and fascinating history. When written history doesn't exist, myth and legend are left to tell the tale. Ruins and other ancient relics only serve to deepen the mystery when uncorroborated by written records. Keep in mind, many of the state's greatest archaeological finds were discovered accidentally. You never can tell. Your next camping trip may be the only expedition necessary to yield the greatest archaeological find in state history.

2 The Spirits Of Oklahoma

I believe everyone loves a good ghost story. It certainly seems like most people know at least one they think may be true. The closer one feels to a person or place involved with a story, the more real it becomes. It seems anyone who hails a claim to a hometown has a local ghost story they swear is true. To list every Oklahoma ghost story I've ever been told would fill a second book. However, some of these ghostly tales are the best (and scariest) I've ever heard. These are the ones you think about when you're all alone, listening to the night wind blowing through the trees. Some ghost stories are just too good to save until Halloween. Tulsa is fortunate enough to be home to, not one, but two famous ghosts. The Gilcrease Museum was established due to the efforts of the late philanthropist, Thomas Gilcrease. After his death in 1962, his spectral image has been seen and heard haunting his labor of love. Gilcrease has also been seen lingering around the Tulsa Historical Society, which was formerly his home.

Tulsa's Brady Theater is said to be haunted by, believe it or not, the ghost of famed virtuoso Enrico Caruso. The great tenor died of pleurisy a year after an open-air ride through the cold, wet Oklahoma outdoors. Caruso's managers blamed his death on that ill-fated stop in Oklahoma. As the story goes, Caruso haunts the Brady Theater as pay back for his untimely demise.

Another haunted theater may be found in Osage County. The Constantine Theater in Pawhuska is said to be haunted by the ghost of Sappho Constantine Brown, daughter of the theater's original owner, Charles A. Constantine. For years, while the old building was being restored, workmen claimed to have heard unexplained footsteps and seen ghostly apparitions.

Ghostly tales from the Cherokee Nation predate statehood, like the one told about a Virginia aristocrat named George M. Murrell. This tale takes place before the Civil War when Oklahoma was Indian territory. Murrell and his Cherokee wife lived in the area around Park Hill. This is the same area he used to fox hunt in the company of friends, aided by a pack of hounds. One night during such a hunt the hounds seemed hot on the trail of something they could not seem to overtake. One of the members of the hunting party was a newspaperman named S.W. Ross. In 1937, he retold the story of that hunt to the *Indian-Pioneer Papers*, an oral history of frontier times. Ross was quoted as saying, "From their excited baying the fast running animals were apparently quite near their object of pursuit." Murrell and his friend James E. Latta were riding onto the pack's trail.

"Major Murrell and Mr. Latta were close together, and upon coming near to the hounds, saw running at great speed, immediately in front of the foremost hounds, a dwarf-like being with long black hair streaming in the early breeze run on a short distance and then suddenly vanished, leaving no trace nor track. Immediately, the hounds lay down, panting and weary." Ross added, "The men stood in awe, unable to believe their eyes." Murrell however took it all in stride saying, "There are some things we do not understand."

It was now dawn. Murrell blew his hunter's horn then lead the awe struck men and weary dogs back towards home.

While driving down a lonely country highway, travelers in Oklahoma may pass right through an area known to be haunted. This could be a stretch of Highway 20, just east of Claremore.

In the winter of 1965, Mae Doria was driving in this location when she gave a ride to a young boy about eleven or twelve years old who was hitch-hiking. The two chatted as they traveled east. Upon reaching Pryor the boy asked to be let out in an area where there were no houses. When Ms. Doria asked him where he lived he replied, "Over there."

She looked to see where he meant and when she turned her head back to the boy he had disappeared! As Ms. Doria recounted the event, "Immediately I stopped the car and, jumping out, ran all around the automobile almost hysterical. I looked everywhere, up and down the highway and to the right and left, but to no avail, he was gone."

In an ironic twist of fate, two years later she was talking to the gas man about psychic experiences. When she mentioned the phantom hitch-hiker the man immediately knew the location. He claimed to have heard tales of a phantom boy hitch-hiker being picked up in that area as far back as 1936.

Some ghosts are not seen, only heard. This disturbing tale of a disembodied voice comes from a cemetery in Arapaho. Since 1972, a voice has been heard calling "Oh no! Oh, my God! Robina has not been saved!"

When the voice first began, it was identified as that of the recently departed George Smith. In 1936, his daughter was killed in a car accident when she was only nineteen. Not only did he never get over her loss, but the fact that she had not achieved salvation haunted him until he was laid to rest next to his wife and daughter. The voice continues to be heard by visitors to the cemetery. In 1980, Cecil and Sharon Rutherford were decorating a nearby grave when they heard, "a deep groan; then a deep masculine voice—very sorrowful—bawled that Robina hadn't been saved." The couple heard it again while about fifty feet from the Smith grave. Thinking it might be a prankster, the two looked around but could see no one.

Even a minister claimed to have heard the voice on March 13, 1979, while holding a funeral service at a nearby grave sight. In an attempt to find a natural explanation, Arthur Turcotte, a geologist who undertakes psychical research in his spare time, studied the grave sight. Not only could he not find a natural explanation but he claims to have clearly heard the voice for himself.

Old structures and other types of settlements with a long history are likely to acquire a ghost or two as time goes by. This is a good description of the ruins of Fort Washita. Located in the Madill-Durant area, Fort Washita was established in 1842 and captured by the rebels during the Civil War. The ruins are said to be haunted by the ghost of a headless woman known as Aunt Jane or Aunt Betsy. As the story goes, the ghost is of an early settler killed by robbers.

After the war the old fort was burned and abandoned. Charles Clobert, a Chickasaw Indian, was lucky enough to be awarded the old site as part of his land allotment from the Chickasaw Nation. The main barracks were rebuilt into a home for him, his family, and his 32 dogs. The first night they moved in, all his dogs disappeared. He spent the next day rounding them up, but the next morning they were gone again. This was enough to convince the Colberts to move back to their townhouse in the city and rent the new home to unsuspecting tenants. One of those tenants who witnessed ghostly goings on was a doctor named Steele. His sister, who kept house for him, suffered a nervous breakdown from the ghostly things she saw. She complained about seeing a woman in the house without a head. Dr. Steele told an early settler named L.L. Sturdivant about a spooky encounter.

According to Sturdivant, "He was alone in the house one night and he was reading a paper. He heard a voice say, 'There's nobody home but just you and me.' On a chair near him sat a big black cat with yellow eyes. Dr. Steele said he ran until he was out of breath, but whenever he stopped there was the cat saying something to him again." The Steeles moved away and no one has lived there since.

The accounts of former residents spread throughout the area. Mrs. N.P. McMinn lived at Fort Washita with her husband who was stationed there during the Civil War. From time to time the McMinns would return to the fort while on outings. It was during one of these visits in 1898 that she met a woman who lived in the ruins of the old fort. She told Mrs. McMinn the story of a terrifying ghostly encounter that occurred one night after supper. The woman was in the kitchen washing dishes when she heard a strange sound that she had heard before; a stone rolling down the roof stopping at the eaves. She paused from her dishwashing and noticed a silvery-white headless figure in the doorway who said to her, "Follow me and I will reward you."

The terrified woman screamed and replied, "I can't, I can't," before fainting. Her husband rushed into the kitchen to find his wife unconscious on the floor.

It is stories like these that keep the old fort area enshrouded in mystery. Because of such tales, ghost-hunting parties have visited the site hoping for (or perhaps dreading) a glimpse of the headless frontier woman.

In the countryside near Cushing in Payne County, about a mile north of the Cimarron River is a spooky spot known as Ghost Hollow. In the late 1800's, the old elm and sycamore trees in the area were ideal for hanging outlaws. According to legend, an innocent man was hanged from an elm tree during the year 1887. The next day, the tree lost all its bark. From that night on, the tree glows an eerie white color in the full moon. This is one of my favorite Oklahoma ghost stories because it has all the right elements: Cowboys, frontier justice, and a lonely, spooky field. The legend of Ghost Hollow is a tale that seems to embrace the true western flavor of Oklahoma's wilder past.

For anyone who would like to visit a ghost, but wouldn't want to live with one, Guthrie's Stone Lion Inn will fit the bill. Built in 1907, the mansion has been converted to a charming bed and breakfast, featuring fine dining and murder mystery weekends. After a while, it became known in a way the innkeepers did not intend.

In 1986, Becky Luker bought the mansion and, with the help of her two sons, Grant and Ral, converted the former funeral home into a cozy, romantic getaway. Soon after moving in the family began hearing the ghostly pitter-patter of little feet, as well as the mysterious sound of a door being opened and closed. After several responses from police yielded no burglary suspects, the family slowly began to accept a more supernatural answer. Two specific areas of ghostly activity are the back staircase between the hours of ten o'clock and midnight, and a big closet on the third floor where the youngest son, Ral, kept his toys. Even though the toys and games were neatly put away and the door locked, the closet's contents would be found scattered on the floor the next morning.

After a while, the Lukers were fortunate enough to be paid a visit by the home's original occupants. Now quite elderly, the trio of Houghton siblings recounted tales from their childhood in order to shed light on the mansion's murky past. F.E. Houghton built the mansion in 1907 and lived there with his family. Although there were many good memories, they told of a sibling who had died. When their sister, Augusta, was eight years old, she had contracted whooping cough. A negligent night maid had given her the wrong kind of medicine, causing Augusta to become violently ill, then die. Could it be the ghost of Augusta Houghton climbing the back staircase, late at night, to play in the toy closet? As the Houghtons would confirm, the Luker boy's toy closet was the same one used by the Houghton children to store their toys, decades earlier. Before her death, Augusta and her siblings would wait until the grown-ups were asleep, then climb the back staircase to the toy room and play. This would usually happen between 10 o'clock and midnight, the same time the Lukers reported hearing prowlers. It would seem the similarities in this case could send a chill down the spine of even the most hardcore of skeptics. In a televised interview, Becky Luker told of four guests who said they were awakened by a hand patting them on the face, but would open their eyes to find no one there. The story of Augusta seems to blend in well with the over-all ambiance of the Stone Lion Inn. The ghost doesn't seem to invoke a feeling of terror (like say for example, a headless frontier woman or a talking black cat), but this may be because no one has actually seen her.

Old buildings tend to collect ghost stories along with dust and cob webs. As we've learned in a few of these ghostly tales, spirits don't always need a building to haunt. It isn't uncommon for ghost stories (as well as the ghosts) to remain attached to an area long after the building is gone. According to Arthur C. Clarke, ghosts are rarely seen by more than one person at a time. Could this mean it's all in our minds? I'll put it this way. Oklahoma is a state with a rich and wild history. So much so, it's bound to be haunted, either in reality, or in the minds of the people who know its colorful past.

3 Strange Sooner Skies

For years I've collected good quality accounts of UFO sightings. By "good quality" I mean reports of sightings involving multiple witnesses, who are hopefully in good standing in their community. After years of studying such cases, I have concluded there is one prerequisite for UFO activity; an airport anywhere in the state. Not only does Oklahoma have its share of both civilian and military airfields, it also has air traffic from all over the country crisscrossing the state. Add that to the fact that natural phenomena such as stars, planets, and lightning can be misidentified as UFOs, and it's easy to see why many Oklahomans have experienced close encounters of the first kind (the sighting of a UFO).

According to air force regulation 200-2, the official definition of a UFO is "any airborne object which by performance, aerodynamic characteristics or unusual features does not conform to any known aircraft."

A typical example of an Oklahoma UFO story would be like the one found on the front page of *The Daily Oklahoman* in late 1987. The headline read, "Unexplained Lights Zoom Across Ponca City Skies." Witnesses reported seeing lights, approximately the shape of light bulbs, racing across the Sooner sky in formations of three and four. One witness claimed they couldn't possibly be from this planet because the objects made no noise. Besides the local residents who witnessed the spectacle, two Ponca City police officers, from different locations, reported seeing a formation of UFOs crossing the sky. To a UFO investigator, this case involved all the right elements to qualify as a high quality report of UFOs, that is, multiple witnesses including law enforcement officials describing the same type phenomenon. Despite the high quality of the facts involved in this case, is it proof of extraterrestrial visitation? No, according to the Federal Aviation Administration, who claimed the bright lights in the sky are common this time of year because of an effect caused by clear and cold atmospheric conditions. In addition, the Ponca City Police Department released a statement a few days later explaining the sightings to actually be three high flying airplanes. Here is an example of honest people, truthfully reporting what they saw, and in no way trying to perpetrate a hoax. This is why there is a need for objective UFO investigation.

During the earlier days of UFO investigation in Oklahoma, a man named Hayden C. Hewes took it upon himself to investigate and organize information on Sooner sightings. In August, 1958, Hewes, with the help of William F. Riefer, organized The International UFO Bureau for the purpose of scientific investigation. Based in Oklahoma, the bureau had over 4000 members nationwide.

In 1965, *Oklahoma's Orbit* published a list of state UFO sightings from the files of The International UFO Bureau. I have reprinted the list (with permission) to provide a historical overview of Oklahoma UFO sightings.

- January, 1924 — A white oval-shaped object lit up the ground before moving out of sight over the horizon.

- June 25, 1947 — A shiny, silvery, round object, very large and high, was reported traveling in an easterly direction at approximately 1200 miles per hour. This was at 8:30 p.m. At 10:30 a.m., two UFOs were reported over Oklahoma City. Pilot Byron Savage reported sighting a disc that sailed over the city and out of sight.
- Early 1950 — A brilliant object was sighted in the sky about 3:30 a.m. by two Edmond police officers. It was described as "white with a long, white tail."
- In 1952 — Mrs. Hugh Ellis, Midwest City, reported a small, bright disc moving parallel to the ground at high speed.
- June 30, 1953 — A highway patrol dispatcher saw something that looked like a shooting star that hovered over Tinker Air Force Base for a long period.
- August 28, 1954 — A formation of fifteen saucers, in triangle formation, was observed by hundreds of citizens at 8:30 p.m. It's reported that Tinker AFB made radar contact. (There's no record of the sighting at Wright-Paterson AFB.)
- August 1955 — M. M. Bulla, attorney, and his family spotted an object while driving along U.S. 270 south of Laverne.
- September 13, 1955 — Dr. Felix Schwartz and his wife watched with other Stillwater residents as a brilliant object with an internal light traveled back and forth over Stillwater at enormous speed.
- October 28, 1957 — Oval shaped object, moving across the sky west of Oklahoma City was reported by a minister.
- In 1957 — UFO sightings were reported all over the state. Seminole and Oklahoma City sightings were dismissed

as F-100 jet fighters. Bethany sightings were passed off as the planet Venus.

• November 9, 1957 — Durant, Madill, Ada and Altus sightings could not be identified.

• November, 1957 — Glenn Northcutt, University board of regents member, sighted an object "like Mars magnified 100 times" while traveling between Blanchard and Chickasha.

• March 3, 1958 — Strange lights sighted over Lake Hefner by many Oklahoma City and Bethany residents at 9 p.m.

• Early 1958 — Lawton and Clinton residents reported a strange light overhead.

• November 12, 1958 — UFOs again returned to Oklahoma City, reported as "lights."

• Late 1958 — Highway patrolman in southwest Oklahoma reported a strange object in the sky.

• February 20, 1959 — Four lights were sighted by Oklahoma City residents including a radio-TV newsman. Objects were reported over Duncan minutes later.

• April, 1959 — Otis T. Carr attempted to launch an "electrogravitational" flying saucer. The OTC X-1 was six feet in diameter, four feet high, weighed about six hundred pounds and cost over $25,000. It never got off the ground.

• May 26, 1959 — An object described as shaped like a lightbulb, but much bigger, was sighted at 8 p.m, over the Arkansas/Oklahoma border.

• July 29, 1960 — A 14-year-old boy reported a "saucer" over Oklahoma City.

- August 31, 1960 — Deputy Director James Maney of The International UFO Bureau and at least two other persons spotted an object over Oklahoma City.
- August 3, 1964 — Countryside near Hugo lit up when a UFO passed overhead. This was seen by many persons.
- September, 1964 — UFO sighted over Oklahoma City at 10,000 feet. It was silver in color. This was the only known UFO to be photographed over Oklahoma. Picture was taken by D. Birmingham.
- September 9, 1964 — Red object sighted traveling west to east overtook an aircraft in approximately ten seconds.
- September 11, 1964 — Car almost hit by "flying saucer" while enroute to Ponca City.
- October 24, 1964 — A blue-violet, round object with a ring of fire around it was reported to El Reno Police at 3 p.m.
- November 6, 1964 — A round UFO was sighted over Oklahoma City by many persons. It landed and was recovered by Rick Barnes. After an intense investigation by the Kirkpatrick Planetarium and the International UFO Bureau, the meteorite was identified as "amygdaloidal melaphyre," the second of its kind ever recovered.
- February 2, 1965 — An object seen hovering high over the northeastern part of Oklahoma City at 7:30 a.m. was described as a silvery ball, appearing about the size of a pea held at arm's length.

On August 2, 1965, the second known photograph of an Oklahoma UFO was taken by a 14-year old paper-boy in Tulsa. It was observed by many witnesses who described watching the craft's tri-colored lights slowly change to a uniform blue-green. The photograph clearly showed what appeared to be an oval-shaped, tri-colored object. It was reviewed by the Condon Committee (a two-year, Colorado University study of the UFO phenomenon, 1966-68) which concluded the photograph was of a large object seen against a background of sky. Although reprinted in a number of publications, no one seems to have the actual photograph. Mr. Hewes, who personally investigated the sighting, lent his copy to *Unsolved Mysteries,* who unfortunately have never returned it.

Although semi-retired, Mr. Hewes still writes and lectures about unexplained phenomena, but leaves the field work to a new breed of investigators.

The Mutual UFO Network (MUFON) is a nationwide grass roots organization, comprised of volunteers who are dedicated to examining the UFO phenomenon. The Oklahoma branch of MUFON investigates between twenty and thirty cases per year. The final reports are sent to the national headquarters in Seguin, Texas for computerization.

"The UFO Mystery" has become a catchall phrase for new phenomena that seems to have a link to UFOs, such as abductions, crop circles and cattle mutilations. Although there is much speculation, few facts exist involving UFOs. One thing for sure, Oklahoma is no stranger to any aspect of the UFO mystery. The strange events occurring in Oklahoma are being reported all over the world. I hope we as a people are strong enough to face the possibility that someday, we may confront undeniable proof that we as a global village, are not alone.

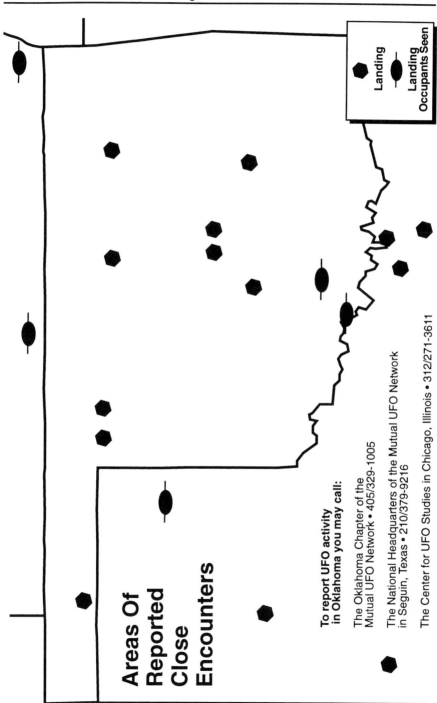

4 Close Encounters Over Ottawa

The most intense period of UFO activity (or "flap" as it's known) in Oklahoma history occurred in the Fall of 1989, beginning approximately October 9. At this time there seemed to be a world-wide UFO flap. Only a few days earlier, Tass, the official Soviet news agency (the former Soviet Union's equivalent to America's Associated Press) announced that scientists had confirmed an alien spaceship carrying giant people with tiny heads had touched down in Voronezh, a city 300 miles southeast of Moscow. This amazing event allegedly occurred September 27, 1989, and was reported in *The Daily Oklahoman* October 11, of the same year. Also appearing in the October 11 issue was an Associated Press story out of Miami, Oklahoma with the heading "Baffling Lights Sighted." Commerce Chief Bob Baine told *The Daily Oklahoman*, "We had received a call about 8:30 p.m. of a UFO around the Brunswick plant, and we thought it was a joke. But when officers arrived on the scene they saw what looked like lights that seemed to move in different directions."

Baine described the spectacle as four lights in a cluster, with a fifth light a short distance away. The police dispatcher said the lights were first reported in Miami and were moving north. This seemed to be supported by a report from a Cherokee County, Kansas, dispatcher who received several calls about the lights in the sky. The lights seemed to have changed after crossing the state line into Kansas when they were then described as three different sets of rotating lights.

The Daily Oklahoman quoted Larry Ruthi, a National Weather Service forecaster, as saying, "A check of area reporting stations indicated no unusual atmospheric conditions that might explain the sightings." This was backed up by Fred Beeler of the National Weather Service who said he knew of no meteorological explanation for the lights. "An auroral display should have been visible over a larger area than just Miami," Ruthi explained. "Frankly I'm at a loss as to what they're seeing." Wayne Wyrick, director and staff astronomer of the Kirkpatrick Planetarium in Oklahoma City, was quoted as saying, "A magnetic storm was sparking an unusually large auroral display in the far north." He doubted the storm was the cause of the lights, but also said he wouldn't rule it out completely."

The Daily Oklahoman ran articles updating the story until October 14. However, local papers were not the only news organizations to take notice of the mysterious lights in the night skies over Ottawa County. *Headline News*, a service of CNN, broadcast a piece encompassing the current worldwide UFO flap. Included in the piece were the Ottawa lights that had been video-taped by a local resident. Although the phenomenon was described as five strange, colored lights, the video tape showed the five lights fused together as one. The television newsmagazine *Hard Copy* also covered the Oklahoma flap. According to one of the witnesses interviewed, "North of our house we saw a craft of some type, it was a triangular shape, it had three white lights and a red one in the middle."

Commerce County Police-Chief Bob Baine not only retold his story for *Hard Copy*, but also was featured in the recreation of the night he, his assistant chief, another Miami police officer, and the mayor, responded to a flood of UFO reports to the police dispatch. Also featured in the news story was footage of the UFO, compliments of KSNF TV.

Regardless of what the lights may have been, they were seen by hundreds of witnesses. Ottawa County played host to nightly star watching parties the week of the sightings. Television and newspaper reporters traveled to the area to see for themselves and to ask questions of local law enforcement agents and other witnesses.

The first officially organized attempt to explain the strange lights occurred Thursday, October 14. Miami and Ottawa County Civil Defense officials and volunteers conducted a four-hour vigil. Volunteers at the Civil Defense command post received twelve phone calls that evening about lights in the sky. The Civil Defense director called the effort "inconclusive."

In an unrelated case eleven years earlier, a similar phenomenon was witnessed approximately eighty miles southwest of Miami. According to the July 1978 issue of the *International UFO Reporter*, two 24 year-old witnesses stargazing with a telescope five miles east of Tulsa reported seeing four grey-white ovals in a fixed formation pass silently in a straight line and moving in a north-easterly direction (which is toward Miami, OK). Each oval appeared about the size of the moon and flew at a 45-degree angle to the direction of travel. The ovals reportedly moved in a sword-like formation with one in the lead and three following. This closely resembled the Miami lights which were described as one light leading and four following. No other sightings were reported to the local police, and nearby Tulsa International Airport failed to report anything. Although this case is of limited merit, it is an interesting coincidence.

The Ottawa County flap of 1989 lasted less than a week. By Monday of the following week, either the lights or the interest in the phenomenon had gone away. However, their origin is still a mystery. Another part of the mystery is that Ottawa County is home to some of the state's elusive "spook lights" (low-level, nocturnal balls of light which seem to dance above the horizon).

Possible explanations have included planets, meteors, reflections caused by atmospheric conditions, or pranks by youngsters using kites or balloons (these events did take place two weeks before Halloween). However, most people who have seen the mysterious lights over Ottawa discount those explanations.

No one is quite sure what people were seeing that week of October, which is why critics claim it must be a hoax. If that were the case, it successfully took in hundreds of local residents and newspapers as well as the Associated Press, CNN, and *Hard Copy* (Oh, O.K., I'll give you that last one).

Does this mean we're dealing with aliens from another world? Since a similar sighting was reported approximately eleven years earlier it would seem that, at the very least, we are dealing with something unknown and very strange.

Personally, I like it better as a mystery. It's arrogant for anyone to believe there is nothing new left in the world to learn. To quote the great scientist, author and visionary, Arthur C. Clarke, "It isn't that our world is more mysterious than we imagine. It's more mysterious than we *can* imagine."

5 The Mysterious Sooner State "Spook Lights"

One of the state's least explained mysteries is the phenomenon of elusive "spook lights" in Northeastern Oklahoma. No one quite knows for sure what they are, but researchers have concluded what they are not. They don't seem to be common lighting because, according to witnesses, there is no sulphur smell. They can't all be airplane lights or the distant headlights of passing cars because the sightings predate these inventions. They do fit the criteria of a UFO, however, they don't appear to be "crafts" under "intelligent" control. The only thing really known is that they appear as low-level, nocturnal balls of lights which seem to dance above the horizon.

Tales of strange lights have also been reported immediately across the borders into Missouri and Arkansas. Because the lights were seen in the area where Oklahoma, Missouri and Arkansas meet, they have been dubbed the Tri-State Spook Lights.

In Loren Coleman's book *Mysterious America*, he published a list, compiled by Mark A. Hall, of 35 recurring spook lights in America. One of the three sites located in Oklahoma is in Tulsa County, two miles west of Sand Springs.

These are apparently the Tri-State Lights, but what about the other two sites?

According to Hall, Cimarron County in the state's panhandle is home to two spook light observatories. Centering around the town of Kenton, one site is to the east eight miles, and the other, fifteen miles to the southwest.

Beaver lies two counties east of Cimarron in the state's panhandle. It is here that William Bathlot claimed he often saw balls of light around his farm. One encounter occurred when Bathlot was returning from Liberal, Kansas, with a wagon-load of lumber. A globe of light frightened the horses, then flew away. In another encounter, Bathlot and a friend were out looking for a lost cow. The men saw a ball of light which moved away as they approached it, and moved towards them as they backed away. Here is Bathlot's account of the incident, compiled from a number of books and magazines.

"Then we just stood there with that thing about a dozen feet in front of us as silent as death itself. It was transparent. We could see a bunch of sage brush right through its body. It hovered in the air approximately eighteen inches above the ground. We could see no body resembling bird or animal, nor could we see anything resembling legs to hold it up. It was just a ball of light."

"Yet apparently this strange object could see us, and it checked our every move. The deadly unnerving stillness of the thing seemed to paralyze us. Finally I raised the shotgun to my shoulder and let it have both barrels. The light went out."

Keith Partain of Tulsa has studied the Tri-State Spook

Lights since 1985. He researched stories about the mysterious balls of light dating as far back as 1880. Partain claims the technicalities of his theory would detract from the romance of the mystery.

"I do believe that it is an independent floating mystery light with some characteristics of ball lightning," Partain said of the Tri-State Lights. "I have a theory of its formation, but I'm saving it to explain it in my book."

In 1977, Marta Poyner-Churchwell took three photos of what Partain believes is a genuine spook light. The pictures (taken in Ottawa County) when viewed in sequence seem to illustrate the light's pattern of movement. The first shows a light with a tail. The light in the second picture appears stationary, and the third picture appears to be a ball of light emitting a daughter ball of light that passes in front of a tree. In 1983, Partain had the Churchwell photos enhanced, although the results were inconclusive.

The U.S. Army Corp of Engineers from Camp Crowder, Missouri, supposedly studied the phenomenon during World War II. Although some newspaper accounts claim the studies were inconclusive, Partain's research could find no evidence of the investigation. He did however find a study conducted in 1946 by the Signal Corps from Camp Crowder. The study showed how the phenomenon could be created with lights. One theory is that the lights could be caused naturally by methane gas (better known as "swamp" gas), however, no sources of methane could be found in the area.

Running west from the Oklahoma/Missouri border is Spook Light Road. Although the lights may be seen from other roads in the area, on Spook Light road are the remains of the Spook Light Museum, formerly owned by Arthur P. "Spooky" Meadows and his brother-in-law, Garland "Spooky" Middleton. Capitalizing on the Spook Light mystery, the two provided a place where the teens could hang out and tourists could be exploited. Since the museum opened in 1960, the lights seem to be a "nightly" mystery, with the legend of the Tri-State Spook Lights remaining quite popular. And anytime you have a lot of people trying to glimpse a mystery, regardless of what the light source, they will swear their sighting was of a "genuine" spook light.

The night skies over Oklahoma are full of wonder and mystery. Each night the moon, stars and planets play various roles in a celestial light show. Occasionally, a lucky observer may witness a falling star, or maybe even a UFO. But only the really lucky will be fortunate enough to catch a glimpse of something as rare and special as an Oklahoma Spook Light.

6 Crop Circles And Landing Sites In The "Wavin' Wheat"

Before the term "crop circles" became so well known, they were simply "alleged landing sites." Long before pictographs in the English wheat fields caught the attention of the world in the late 1980's, investigations of flattened vegetation associated with UFO sightings were serious business. Ted Phillips of Sedelia, Missouri is recognized as the world's leading authority on this subject. As a Research Associate of the Center for UFO Studies, he has investigated over 1480 landing sites from 59 countries. Four hundred of the cases studied involved more than one witness observing a craft for longer than one minute, at distances of less than 250 feet. Most of the cases in Phillips' files involve an alarming number of consistencies. Usually the affected area is in the shape of a disc and between 10 to 35 feet in diameter. This sounds similar to the crop circles appearing in the wheat fields of England, however, after looking at the facts, it appears we may be dealing with two different mysteries.

Colin Andrews has examined the crop circle mystery in England since 1980 and is considered the world's top authority. According to his research, in cases involving "genuine" crop circles, the stalks of the vegetation are not broken but merely laid to the side and allowed to continue growing. According to Andrews the hoaxers who create such circles trample the crops flat, breaking the stalks. In the cases examined by Ted Phillips the vegetation in the ring is usually dead and the affected soil does not support future plant life.

Although these mysteries appear different, they do share some characteristics, the most common being patches of electromagnetic energy within the rings in some cases. In one crop circle found in England a strange "energy" type sound was recorded and felt at the same time by a sound technician. It is the opinion of many researchers that UFOs are powered by electromagnetic energy.

In the early nineties, the crop circle phenomenon became almost world-wide. Here again, I believe the line separating landing sites and crop circles may have become blurred, which could account for the rise in numbers. Of course, the soil and crops of the English countryside are different than that of other parts of the world, so the same phenomena may appear different.

In 1991, the semi-arid terrain of Oklahoma was marked with strange circles of its own. Although alleged landing sites had been found before in the state, the popularity of the subject caused Oklahoma to receive international attention.

The state chapter of the Mutual UFO Network (MUFON) investigated circles found in Edmond, Fargo, and Norman. Actually, there were two cases in the Norman area that seem to be chemically related. Jean Waller of Oklahoma MUFON told the *Oklahoma Gazette*, "The cause is undetermined, but we suspect some sort of chemical infestation." Bear in mind that Norman (as well as Edmond) is a college town, so I wouldn't rule out intoxicated fraternity members as a potential source.

The crop circles found near Fargo were the second UFO related story from Oklahoma in a two year period to be picked up by the Associated Press. Floyd Steinert and his wife Dorothy first noticed the strange circles in their rye field on Father's Day, June 16, 1991. Two circles, one measuring 25 feet and the other 31 feet in diameter, were found approximately 200 yards apart. A third circle measuring 10 feet across, described as more of a soil discoloration, was found not far away. The three circles formed a triangular pattern with two points marking a direct east-west line.

"The really odd part is that the electromagnetic energy field is equal in both," Waller told the *Oklahoma Gazette*. "The lines cross right smack-dab in the middle of each circle." The energy fields were determined by the use of metal rods that would cross at certain points within the circles.

UFO organizations weren't the only ones interested in the Fargo crop circles. Glenn Schickendanz, manager of the Farmer's Co-op in Fargo, visited the site along with the county extension agent. The men didn't see a third circle, but did see that something had caused the vegetation to die in the two circles. Soil samples taken from the field indicated no difference between samples taken in and outside of the ring. According to *The Daily Oklahoman*, Ellis County extension director R.A. Devore said, "A soil test he made at the site failed to show what caused the basically bare ground within the circles." Another interesting fact about the circles is that none of the researchers reported finding footprints at any of the sites. Although crop circles in England have been seen in the making, no one knows how they are made or who is making them. Strange lights in the sky are often observed in the areas where the circles have been found. When the rings were found at Fargo, a few of its residents recounted old tales of UFOs.

Floyd Steinert, in the same article, said he was "just as much at a loss as anybody. I've never seen anything like this before, and I've been farming all my life. Personally I find it hard to think that they were caused by a UFO, but so many people have said they've seen them, I'd be the last one to call them liars." Two of the witnesses are his wife and daughter.

Several years ago, Dorothy Steinert claimed to have seen strange lights in the area. This account can hardly compare to one told by daughter Joyce Wade about a UFO she claimed to have witnessed in 1957 when she was sixteen.

Approximately two months after the rings were found, Wade told her story to Jim Etter of *The Daily Oklahoman*. According to the article, it was late in the day when, "A large, silver object, without engines, wings, lights or sound, passed about 100 feet over her." It then turned and came back, flying directly over her head. Wade said her sister Janet caught a glimpse of the object as it rose out of sight, but thought it was a weather balloon.

Wade, who's husband Steve is the local Police Chief, feared ridicule, so she kept it to herself. It was after the discovery of the mysterious rings when she gained the courage to let her story be known.

A few months after the circles were found, the vegetation returned. The circles began to fade, just like the strange tales they've inspired.

Crop Circles And Landing Sites In The Wavin' Wheat 53

Oklahoma MUFON investigators taking careful measurements of a circular formation in a field near Shawnee, Oklahoma.

Photos Courtesy of Oklahoma MUFON.

Oklahoma MUFON State Director Jean Waller Seifried takes notes at the crop circle sight. The edge of the formation can be clearly seen on the right.

Under the umbrella of the UFO mystery, additional mysteries have been discovered. Saucer crashes, abductions, government cover ups and now crop circles are only a few of the various aspects of the investigation. It seems the more we learn, the more questions we accumulate go unanswered. As much as I'd like to learn the secrets of all these mysteries, I realize life without mystery would be very boring; but don't worry about that ever happening. As long as we continue to explore the world around us, there will never be a shortage of mysteries.

7 Oklahomans And Alien Abductions

Of all the mysteries associated with UFO phenomena, alien abduction is, in my opinion, both the scariest and hardest to believe. It's natural for people to have occasional nightmares, especially when under stress or after a traumatic experience. We usually awaken, relieved to discover it wasn't real. However, for some people, the fear remains as they remember a dream that seems too real. Could these images be attributed to the subconscious working out its anxiety in our dream world in order to keep us mentally healthy? If that is its purpose, it seems to be doing just the opposite. The abductees I've met share in common a genuine sense of fear when discussing their experiences. As if the fear weren't enough, try to imagine the frustration of recalling events you know are impossible, but seem too real to be simply dreams or imagination. Then think of trying to explain it to someone else. None of this proves they were kidnapped by extraterrestrials, but it has convinced me that most of these people have been traumatized by something, whether real or imagined. Because I remain skeptical, the purpose of this chapter is to provide the reader with what is known about abduction phenomena. Although I refer to abduction cases involving Oklahomans, they vary little from similar incidents reported worldwide. I also want the reader to understand, I am not trying to be blasphemous or change anyone's view of religion or the world, I am only presenting the information as I found it.

During the 1980's, there was an explosion of people claiming long repressed events remembered through the use of hypnotherapy. Most of these cases involved traumatic events, usually experienced during early childhood. In cases involving what has become known as "missing time" the same technique was used to help the patient recall what the conscious mind couldn't remember. There exists extensive documentation of many of these cases by noted researchers of varying credentials. According to their research, many of these people experiencing periods of missing time had been abducted by aliens, taken aboard spaceships, given medical examinations, and before being returned, had the experience blocked from memory. It sounds too incredible to believe. But what exactly were these people recalling? Hypnosis is not a truth serum. It could be possible these people were recalling events from dreams, movies, or other peoples tales of alien encounters.

In the early 1990's, "false memory syndrome," became popular. According to both psychiatrists and attorneys, the syndrome was responsible for bizarre memories and false accusations. If you didn't like that explanation, you could blame the abduction experiences on sleep paralysis, more commonly known as a waking dream. In such a case, a person is coming out of a state of sleep, but is still dreaming and may be unable to move their body. This could explain the sensation of paralysis abductees describe when recalling their experiences. There are also medical and psychological disorders, such as narcolepsy and schizophrenia, which may account for hallucinations.

Having listed my reasons for being skeptical, I will now explain why I am so fascinated by this mystery. There are many popular cases involving alien abductions, or as they've come to be known, Close Encounters of the Fourth Kind. The two most popular cases involved Betty and Barney Hill (1961) and Travis Walton (1975). Both cases were extensively investigated by a number of researchers and, as you might have guessed, both cases were eventually made in to movies (Hill's: *The Interrupted Journey*, Walton's: *A Fire In The Sky*).

In 1987, Budd Hopkins' book, *Intruders*, hit the best-sellers list as a follow up to his earlier book, *Missing Time*. It told the incredible story of people who were abducted numerous times throughout their lives and were forced to participate in genetic experiments. As unbelievable as the accounts may be, Hopkins' evidence to support his claims was quite convincing. He notes how in many cases, people who never met can tell almost the exact same story, including many specific details. The next best-seller to document alien abductions received a lot of attention, not only because of the subject, but because of who wrote it. Dr. David Jacobs, Associate Professor of History at Temple University, was the first researcher of such outstanding accreditation to admit the abduction phenomena, whatever is causing it, does exist. In his book, *Secret Life*, Dr. Jacobs' study of alleged "abductees" seems to validate the findings of Hopkins.

John E. Mack, M.D., a Professor of Psychiatry at Harvard Medical School and Pulitzer Prize winner, wrote the forward to Dr. Jacobs' book. Dr. Mack later wrote his own book, *Abduction: Human Encounters with Aliens*, which described his work with abductees. Both Jacobs and Mack risked their professional reputations to bring their findings to the public. On a more local note, Psychologist Dr. Larry McCauley, in an interview with KWTV reporter Kelly Ogle gave his opinion, "I'm trying to look at it with a reasonably open mind...the research, and it's good research, seems to indicate there's something there to pay attention to." Dr. McCauley's statement was in reference to the abduction phenomenon during a local news story on the subject.

A number of Oklahomans have been involved in the phenomenon of alien abductions, not only as researchers, but as the subjects themselves. Jean E. Byrne is a registered nurse and massage therapist, as well as a hypnotherapist for the Oklahoma chapter of the Mutual UFO Network (or "MUFON" as they're commonly called). She said she had worked on about twenty abduction cases involving Oklahomans. One case involved an Oklahoma City attorney who Byrne and MUFON have kept anonymous. In the mid-sixties he worked as a surveyor in a national forest of the Pacific Northwest. One night while camping in a largely unpopulated section of forest, he experienced something unusual; as he slept under the stars, the moon rose and shone so hot he had to kick off his covers. He later realized he could not account for several hours after sighting the "hot moon."

For years the man suffered from what could best be described as post-traumatic stress syndrome, although no memory of an event existed. According to Byrne, the man contacted MUFON after seeing Whitley Striber's book, *Communion*. The depiction of the cover's bulbous eyed creature suddenly caused the man to shake uncontrollably with fear. The cover of the book featured a space alien Striber claims to have encountered during his own abduction experiences.

Byrne said it took many sessions before the man could remember his own period of missing time. She asked the man to look behind a curtain where he would see what had happened. The man responded he couldn't because "they" had told him not to. Finally he did look, after being convinced what had happened to him was against the law. The man was then able to tell his story of what could best be described as a typical (if there is such a thing) alien abduction experience.

The hot moon he remembered was actually some kind of spacecraft. He was immobilized, then floated inside the craft by beings who looked like the creature on the cover of Striber's book. He was then physically examined, telepathically interrogated, and had semen extracted by some type of "device." When his abductors finished with him, he was returned to his camp, then "programmed" not to tell anyone about the experience.

Byrne said a number of forest service workers have shared similar experiences, "They're perfect subjects, alone in the wilderness and away from witnesses."

Another abduction case MUFON investigated was that of Norman resident, Richard Seifried. A retired high school social studies teacher and former forest ranger, Seifried was not known for practical jokes. He simply tried to understand what happened to him.

On July 15, 1977, Seifried was working at a National Forest in Idaho. He was walking up a hill to a look-out station. "I heard what sounded like electric horns, like you hear at a basketball game. Then there was a strange roar and I heard trees crashing," he said. Puzzled by the sound, he continued up the mountain. Suddenly he felt strangely tired. "The woman who ran the station took one look at me and asked what had happened. That's when I discovered I was very dehydrated." During his stay at the station the woman mentioned there had been several recent UFO sightings in the area. Seifried gulped fluids and rested until he felt strong enough to head back down the mountain. On the way he intended to check out the area where he heard the strange sounds. When he began his descent something strange happened. "Suddenly I was three miles away from where I thought I was and it was later in the day than it should have been. But something kept bothering me," Seifried recalled. "Finally, in 1981 when I was in Dayton, Ohio, without telling anyone what I was doing, I found a doctor and went under regressive hypnosis."

Under hypnosis he told the doctor about that day in July, how he had been abducted by aliens not once, but twice. Further hypnosis sessions revealed he had first been abducted in 1947, when he was in the wilderness, alone, hiking at a YMCA camp in Ohio.

Richard Seifried was the Assistant State Director in charge of investigations for Oklahoma MUFON until 1994. As a multiple abductee, he is still active in MUFON, and helps others who may have shared similar experiences.

One of Seifried's latter encounters with aliens occurred in

1990, while camping at Black Mesa in Oklahoma. He described his Black Mesa encounter, as well as other cases investigated by Oklahoma MUFON in a book he coauthored with Michael S. Carter, entitled *Native Encounters*. I met with both gentlemen and read their book. I found them to be honest hard working members of their communities, who try to enlighten others concerning UFO phenomena.

Emotional scarring is not the only evidence of alien abductions. Many abductees have reported mysterious puncture-like wounds they have no memory of ever receiving. The wounds reported could be compared to those left by various medical examining procedures. Many of these wounds seem to heal in a similar manner, leaving small, round indentations in the skin, commonly referred to as "scoop marks" by abduction researchers. In some cases, inorganic pieces of material have been removed from the skin of abductees, although there is no memory of any event that would explain how it got there. This is an example of something that isn't proof of alien abductions, but does seem to deepen the mystery.

There exists a condition in which the mind can cause the skin to form wounds and bleed known as stigmata. It is usually associated with religion because of the followers of Christ who have been documented to spontaneously bleed from wounds similar to the ones suffered by Christ during his crucifixion. Although stigmata could be a possible explanation in some cases, it usually doesn't leave scars and cannot account for any objects found under the skin.

Linda Moulton Howe is an Emmy award-winning television producer and author. She is also considered the top authority on the mutilation of cattle and its connection to the UFO mystery (see following chapter). Howe claims to have seen privileged information from classified government documents presented to her by high ranking members of the United States Military. In her book, *An Alien Harvest*, Howe claims the cattle mutilation mystery and the alien abduction mystery are related. She explained that both mysteries involve alien intelligence conducting genetic experiments, all with the knowledge of the government. On the other side of the spectrum, in *Secret Life*, Dr. Jacobs listed twenty potential answers to the abduction phenomena that could explain how a person could be lead to believe they had been abducted by aliens, when in actuality they had not. Personally, I believe the truth is somewhere between these two extremes. I find it interesting that both Howe and Dr. Jacobs have concluded that aliens are not here to help mankind, but to exploit it. If that isn't scary enough, bear in mind these aliens apparently have the technology to perform their tasks while remaining unseen until they decide to reveal themselves.

Some researchers have pointed out the similarities between alien abductors, and biologists who trap wild animals to study in order to understand how they live. Others note fairy tales involving gnomes, leprechauns and other types of "magical" little people and their likeness to alleged descriptions of extraterrestrial humanoids. Although I have drawn no definite conclusions concerning alien abductions, I am trying to remain open minded about the subject while collecting information from both sides of the argument.

I believe most people who claim to be abductees are truly

suffering from something and only want answers to their questions. If the entire abduction phenomenon turns out to be the result of mental illness or just an over-active imagination, it would certainly make a lot of people feel better.

I wish there were a more optimistic conclusion to reassure the reader. However, the information I reviewed to prepare this chapter seemed to suggest two possibilities; some type of psychological abnormality is to blame, or aliens are abducting human specimens for their own selfish reasons and there is nothing anyone can do to stop them. Sweet dreams.

Two photos of mutilated cows found in Oklahoma. Incisions indicate exposure to high heat in excess of 350 degrees, which could be equated to the use of modern laser surgery.

Photos courtesy of Oklahoma MUFON.

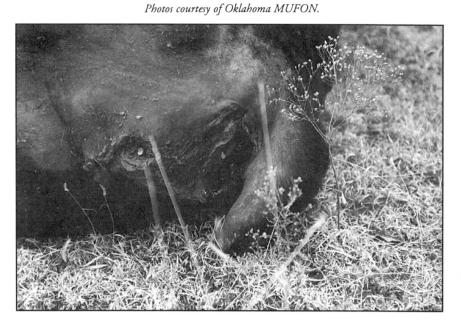

8 Mysterious Mutilators

You need only play "count the cows" during an extended road trip through Oklahoma to realize you're in the heart of cattle country. The large herds of livestock represent an investment of much time and money. The ranchers do their best to safeguard their investment from loss to predators, rustlers and disease. Unfortunately just like any business, there can be losses that are beyond the control of the stockholders.

Since the late 1960's ranchers have occasionally discovered cattle killed and mutilated under unusual circumstances. Cows are usually the focus of the mystery but many types of livestock have been involved. A description of a typical mutilation would be a dead animal found with various body parts missing, such as one eye or one ear and the tongue. Usually the sex organs of the animal are removed and the rectum is cored out with surgical precision. The hides of the animals usually show large "cookie cutter" type holes seemingly punched out of the carcass. Despite all the wounds the death scene is usually void of blood and footprints. It would seem the assailants either "floated" while draining the animal of blood or through some aerial means, abducted the animal, conducted various medical procedures, then dropped the carcass to the pasture below. Many reported mutilations can be explained by predators or other natural occurrences. Flying scavengers with sharp beaks feed on a carcass then fly away, which could explain the lack of footprints. Insects known as "blow flies" pick over wounds made by other predators thereby cleaning up ragged edges and creating the impression of "surgical precision." The lack of blood at the scene could be explained by the fact that when an animal dies and then falls on its side, the blood drains to the lowest parts of the body where it coagulates and then evaporates. On the other hand there are aspects to the cattle mutilation mystery that are not so easily explained.

The era of cattle mutilations in America began in 1967 in Colorado. A three-year-old Appaloosa named "Lady" (erroneously called "Snippy" in a number of reports) appeared frisky and healthy on the evening of September 7. The following morning Lady was found dead, lying on her left side, with the flesh above her shoulders stripped away to the skull, leaving nothing but bone. As if this weren't strange enough, no tracks, not even that of the horse, could be found within a one-hundred foot radius of the carcass. Further investigation revealed some internal organs had also been removed. Doctors, investigators and skeptics in general offered a variety of explanations. Two points I believe were not adequately explained pertain to the large amount of physical damage in such a short period of time and the lack of any footprints.

During the 1970's mysterious cattle mutilations were being reported throughout the mid and southwest states to as far north as Montana. Whether it was just mass hysteria or a bonafide national conspiracy is still unclear, however one thing was certain; a genuine climate of concern existed within the cattle raising community. Cattle associations, lawmen and even senators were hounded by ranchers demanding that something be done. By the end of the 1970's public outcry became so intense as to require congressional hearings in an attempt to solve the mystery. Senator Harrison Schmitt of New Mexico convened a public hearing in Albuquerque during the spring of 1979. As a result, $44,000 in tax payer's money was obtained from the U. S. Law Enforcement Assistance Administration to fund an investigation.

Throughout the year of the investigation, 27 alleged mutilation cases were investigated and 90 earlier cases were reviewed. At the end of the year Kenneth M. Rommel, Jr., a former FBI agent who headed the investigation, concluded that all the mutilations he investigated were "consistent with what one would expect to find with normal predation, scavenger activity, and normal decomposition of a dead animal." He believed this to be true for "a good many of the other mutilations." This helped quiet the mutilation mystery for a while, but still left some unanswered questions, such as the fate of Lady and other similar cases. Fifteen years later Pete Domenici would become the next senator from New Mexico to investigate the cattle mutilation mystery. He officially asked the state Livestock Board to share with him what it had learned about Northern New Mexico cattle mutilations. In a letter to Board Director John Wortman, Senator Domenici stated he was prepared to ask the federal government for whatever resources were necessary. Apparently the board determined the mutilations were not being caused by predators.

Oklahoma has been affected by the cattle mutilation mystery since the early 1970's. Mutilations in the Sooner State do not occur as frequently as others, but the loss to the cattle rancher is still great. Regardless of the state in which they occur, authorities have concluded that a large number of mutilated cattle are the result of satanic cults (yes, they *do* exist in Oklahoma). Usually cattle mutilations are associated with aerial phenomena, however the down to Earth explanation of cult activity must also be investigated.

During the month of January in 1992, a number of cattle deaths in northern Oklahoma originally blamed on coyotes was believed to be the work of a satanic cult. Grant County Sheriff Archie Yearick began investigating the possibility of cult activity after a veterinarian confirmed that the most recent cow was mutilated by humans. Yearick told *The Daily Oklahoman* that cult members kill and mutilate cattle for holiday rituals. "There are 26 satanic holidays a year, with most months having two holidays," Yearick said. "Animal and human blood and each organ have different meanings."

Between August of 1991 and January 1992 five heifers were found dead and mutilated in specific ways. The parts of the cows taken, such as sexual organs, eyes, ears and the tongue, match those parts needed for specific types of satanic rituals near the time the mutilations took place. Three of the carcasses were found in the northeastern part of Grant County not far from the Kansas border and the other two were found around the town of Medford. The following week six were found, three in Garfield County which borders Grant County on the south, and three in Kingfisher County which boarders Garfield to the north. The Friday before the cattle were found was a satanic holiday known as "satanic revels." *The Daily Oklahoman* reported that Garfield County authorities suspected a "satanic house" to be in the area where one mutilated carcass was the six were heifers, and one of the mutilations in Garfield County involved a bull. It was difficult to find any tracks because the mutilations had occurred days earlier. Ranchers were told by authorities to keep a close watch on their cattle and to be on the lookout for any suspicious vehicles or persons in the area.

After only a couple of weeks authorities abandoned their investigation of any cult connection to the mutilated cattle (at least publicly). Kingfisher County Sheriff Danny Graham told *The Daily Oklahoman* that it appeared the cattle had died from natural causes, based on tests conducted on tissue samples from only one of the animals by Oklahoma State University's veterinary medicine pathology laboratory. Authorities suspected the cattle could have been killed with dart guns loaded with powerful muscle relaxers which they claimed was a common practice of satanic worshippers. According to Graham, the tests showed no barbituates or tranquilizers in the cows' tissue and deputies found no evidence at the scene that the cow had been shot, "It just died," he said. "There's no physical evidence to establish satanic ritual activity based on the results of the medical examination." Since the condition of the other two carcasses was similar, officers concluded all three had died of natural causes, although only parts of the one cow were tested.

Towards the end of 1992, lawmen again found themselves investigating mutilated cattle in the neighboring counties of Comanche and Tillman. On June 16, Comanche County Sheriff Kenny Stradley made a grizzly discovery in a pasture six miles west of Lawton. A pregnant cow was found with its eyeballs, heart and rear end removed, and the unborn calf pulled out of its mother's body and "cut up," according to Stradley.

"Whoever did it knew exactly what they were looking for. They were very clean cuts, like from a scalpel," he added.

Approximately one week prior to the September 7th satanic celebration known as the "marriage to beast/satan" holiday, a mutilated cow was found in a pasture northeast of Tipton. The Oklahoma Cattlemen's Association offered a $5000 reward for information leading to the arrest and conviction of the people involved. In November 1990, authorities in the counties of Comanche and Tillman reported similar crimes. In a pasture seven miles west of Grandfield, a three-week-old calf was found stripped of its flesh and entrails. No blood was found at the scene. Squares and circles of hide had been cut out, and the rest was pulled over its head. About the same time, a skinned calf was found in rural Comanche County. So far, the $5,000 reward offered by the Oklahoma Cattlemen's Association remains unclaimed.

When facts are uncovered which logically explain a mystery, the case is usually closed. It isn't because the police are sloppy, but because unfortunately, they are unable to spend all their time and resources guarding cattle. Law enforcement officials have recently found an alliance with a civilian organization whose members are equally interested in solving the cattle mutilation mystery. The Mutual UFO Network (or MUFON as they're known) is interested in learning the connection between cattle mutilations and unusual aeriel activity. One characteristic of mutilations involving UFOs is that the incisions appear to have been created by the use of high-intensity heat, similar to laser surgery. Bear in mind this aspect of the mutilation mystery was first reported long before laser technology had been developed. Although authorities may not flaunt the fact,

Oklahoma MUFON and law enforcement have shared information involving many types of cases. One of the reasons this grassroots UFO organization has been so successful in gathering information is because the members guarantee confidentiality in all cases and will not release any names to the public or media. Members of Oklahoma MUFON may investigate many alleged cattle mutilations before finding one with a UFO connection. But they do find them.

When MUFON investigators are fortunate enough to find a mutilated animal before too much deterioration has occurred, tissue samples are sent to Dr. John Henry Altshuler, M.D., an assistant Clinical Professor of Medicine (Hematology) and Pathology at the University of Colorado Health Sciences Center in Denver. According to Oklahoma MUFON, there were seven known mutilated cows in 1992; one near Broken Arrow, another east of Oklahoma City, and five in a north-south line extending from the Kansas boarder to Caddo County.

Chuck Pine, an investigator for Oklahoma MUFON, is familiar with the majority of the mutilation cases. On February 3, 1992, Pine visited Garfield, Kingfisher and Grant counties to collect information about the cattle mutilations and to offer assistance via the resources of MUFON. He was informed of a freshly mutilated cow in Caldwell, Kansas, just about two miles north of the Oklahoma border. Caldwell, Kansas is only a few miles north of Medford, Oklahoma, and seems to be part of the northwest line of mutilated cattle running through Oklahoma. The lawman involved was glad to see the investigator and took him to meet the farmer who owned the cow. Pine photographed the area where the farmer found the dead cow, minus the carcass which had been moved. Tissue samples were taken from the animal's cheek, tongue, stomach and rectal areas. The samples were sent to Dr. Altshuler who, after examining the tissue, determined that, "high heat had been applied in making the incisions." This case is just one of many investigated and documented by Oklahoma MUFON, but certainly not the most dynamic.

On the morning of February 6, 1992, a mutilated cow was found by a farmer and his son on their property in the town of Medford. That same evening at about 8:00 pm, the son of the farmer and his girlfriend were driving toward the farm. When they were about two miles away, they noticed a light hovering over the site of the morning's mutilation. As they got closer, they could see that the light was a "craft" of some kind. It was described as a saucer type object with green, red, yellow, and white lights around the outer edge that would blink in no particular sequence. The young man wanted to get a closer look, but his girlfriend was afraid, so he agreed to take her home. As the two drove towards town they noticed the craft was in pursuit. Although they traveled at speeds up to eighty miles an hour they couldn't lose the strange object. Upon reaching town, the object kept going and passed them. The youth and his father returned to the field where the craft had been sighted. They could see the lights of the craft about a mile out of town and noticed it seemed to be headed back to their land. As the men drove closer, they could see the craft hovering over their field. In order to avoid a confrontation, the farmer drove two miles past the object, then turned around. When they returned, the object was gone but could be seen flying southeast until out of sight.

On the following Monday afternoon of February 10, a second cow was found mutilated in a manner similar to the first one. Tissue samples from both cows were sent to Dr. Altshuler in Colorado, who determined that the wounds were inflicted by knives and showed no evidence of "high heat." Circumstantial evidence would suggest UFO's were involved, but there was no real proof linking the two. The UFO connection in this case is interesting, but the physical evidence would suggest humans were to blame.

Although 1992 was a particularly busy year in terms of cattle mutilations in Oklahoma, the mystery has not been satisfactorily solved and mutilations continue to occur. In late April 1993, two mutilated black cattle were found in fields about sixty miles apart, following a full moon. The 1,100-pound Angus cow found in Mustang and the 700-pound Angus steer found near Hydro both had sex organs removed. The tongue and one eye from each animal had also been removed along with a patch of hide from the cow. A few drops of blood were found at the scenes but none appeared to have come from the cuts. Equally as strange, no tracks, human or animal, could be found despite the soft ground from recent rains. The cause of death was undetermined in both cases. Neither animal was sick and a local veterinarian couldn't find any bullet holes. The wounds were determined to have been made by knives, hinting at an unknown human assailant. There were no suspects, and few questions have been answered. What does exist is a mysterious tale that will be retold by many people, prompting listeners to draw their own conclusions.

Mysteriously mutilated cattle have appeared in Oklahoma but not as often as other parts of the country. Predators and crazed cultists may be to blame in a minority of the cases, but it doesn't seem likely that they could account for some of the more bizarre clues that have been found.

Not all mutilation researchers believe UFOs are to blame, but that doesn't mean mysterious forces are not at work. In some cases dark colored helicopters were observed in the same areas as recent mutilations. The so called "black helicopters" have been reported all across America beginning sometime in the late 1970's. During this same time rumors began to spread claiming the military had accidentally contaminated certain areas of the country and that animals were being secretly examined in order to determine if there were any effects. This premise was used in two movies, *Rage* and *Endangered Species*, to account for waves of mysteriously killed cattle. Many conspiracy theorists claim these helicopters were used in a variety of covert government operations. Perhaps the mysterious black helicopters are actually the latest urban (or in this cases "rural") legend to be invented. However, legends usually have their roots in reality.

During the early 1990's black military style helicopters were reported around the town of Fyffe, Alabama, where an intense wave of cattle mutilations occurred. Witnesses saw helicopters flying at tree top level and in some cases the aircraft carried beneath it a "box" which appeared large enough to hold a cow. Law enforcement officials and other investigators in Fyffe described the same elements found in Oklahoma and across the country; a bloodless scene with no footprints, not even that of the animals.

Some researchers claim the United States Government was responsible for the mutilated cattle being found, some say it's UFOs and some believe both have a hand in it.

Linda Moulton Howe first began her investigative research of bizarre animal deaths on September 1, 1979, when she worked as a Director of Special Projects at the CBS television affiliate in Denver, Colorado. Ms. Howe, who would later win an Emmy, is a talented producer, director and writer who was already enjoying the fruits of a successful career. It would seem the last thing she needed was to get mixed up with UFOs.

When she started work on her documentary *A Strange Harvest,* she thought she would uncover the cause of the animal deaths and that it would point to accidental contamination of the environment by the government. What she found was one "off the record story" after another about UFOs being seen in the area of the mutilations. Her environmental documentary then became an accumulation of human testimony that suggested the presence of extraterrestrial mutilators.

After *A Strange Harvest* was first aired on May 25, 1980, Ms. Howe received hundreds of phone calls and letters from people claiming to have had similar experiences. In 1982, Ms.Howe signed a contract with Home Box Office (HBO) to produce a documentary that was to be called *UFOs: The E.T. Factor.* From this point Ms.Howe drifted from conventional journalism to a world of classified government information, incredible tales of human contact with alien intelligence and government sources not making good on their promises.

The heart of the investigation began at the Air Force Office of Special Investigations (AFOSI) at Kirkland Air Force Base in Albuquerque, New Mexico. Air Force Officials had been told there was a documentary in the works and were expecting Ms. Howe. In her book *An Alien Harvest,* Ms. Howe alleges an AFOSI agent gave her some papers to read entitled "Briefing

Paper for the President of the United States of America." The paper concerned crashed alien crafts and the recovery of extraterrestrial biological entities, both dead and alive. The paper went on to describe ongoing communications between the grey-skinned aliens (or "greys") and the United States Government dating back to the 1940's. The paper also described alien intervention as responsible for the genetic manipulation of life here on Earth, and that cattle mutilations and human abductions by these aliens were a means of monitoring the progress of their work. Ms. Howe claims she was told by the agent that the government had decided to inform the public about contact with extraterrestrials. Additionally, she was to be provided with thousands of feet of "historic" UFO film footage. As it turned out the government agent never made good on his promises and without the film in question, HBO decided to cancel the documentary.

Perhaps the overall intention of the government was to either sabotage the documentary or to discredit Ms. Howe, whose investigation was getting too close for their comfort.

Linda Moulton Howe has continued her investigation ever since and has become the leading authority in the field of cattle mutilations and their connection with UFOs. The result of her years of research do not yield comforting implications. In fact, it seems to suggest at least one form of alien intelligence is responsible for mutilating cattle and abducting humans for genetic research, all with the knowledge of the United States Government and there is nothing any of us earthlings can do to stop them.

Personally, I don't agree with all the implications of this controversial investigation, but I will concede the findings of Ms.

Howe indicate the presence of a real mystery, as opposed to a compilation of events easily explained away.

Not everyone who has investigated the cattle mutilation mystery has drawn the same conclusions as Linda Howe, MUFON or a variety of state cattlemen's associations. Even the Center for UFO Studies expressed doubts concerning whether or not a real mystery even exists. Lawmen have suggested the lack of footprints could be explained by cultists walking on sheets of cardboard and psychologists have suggested the whole mystery is a result of mass hysteria.

Another aspect to this mystery could be insurance fraud. In some cases cattle are insured against vandalism, however, if the animal dies of natural causes the death is not covered. The problem I have with these nay sayers is that it seems for every case they explain away there still remain cases they can't. The use of lasers, the sightings of military style helicopters, and the hundreds of UFOs reported during the waves of mutilation activity have led me to accept there is more at work here than just predators and crazed cultists.

The cattle mutilations seem to fit within the realm of human abductions by aliens and the mysterious formation of crop circles. These mysteries seem connected because they all routinely occur at night, unseen by witnesses. They hint at an "unseen world" coexisting with what we know as the "real world." It conjures the old philosophical question; if a tree falls in the forest and there is no one there to hear it, does it make a sound? I don't know of anyone working on the "tree sound mystery," however investigators across the country, in addition to MUFON, will continue to examine the mystery of cattle mutilations and other such enigma until an answer is found.

9 Mysterious Cats And Other Strange Four-Legged Creatures

Outdoorsmen in Oklahoma usually have little to fear from ferocious animals. Although the Department of Wildlife Conservation has officially recognized populations of black bear and cougars, confrontations with humans are rare. On even rarer occasions Oklahomans have encountered species of big cats and other large predators not known to live in the state, let alone the country. Some of these accounts are so bizarre it seems either the witnesses are lying, or there are strange creatures stalking the Sooner State. When dealing with such stories, the source of the information is usually brought into question, however some sources are quite credible. In March, 1961, *Newsweek Magazine* published an article pertaining to Oklahoma entitled, "Lion at Large." A tourist from Ohio first saw the lion while driving along the Will Rogers Turnpike. He told an attendant at the next exit that he had seen an "unmistakable African lion" prowling in a field along the roadside. The article quoted the unnamed traveler as having asked, "Say, what kind of animals do you people have in Oklahoma?" Within 24 hours the lion was again spotted in the same general vicinity of Big Cabin. Two nurses at the Oklahoma State Hospital reported seeing what they thought was a large dog in the shrubbery.

After a second look, one of the nurses cried, "That's not a dog, it's a lion!" The two nurses then beat a hasty retreat.

It was later learned the beast in question was prowling in the area approximately two months prior to the sightings (January, 1961). The majority of sightings occurred in the Big Cabin area. Some residents, who didn't actually see the lion, found tracks and heard it roar. One farm woman reported some of her livestock had been killed and eaten. She later photographed tracks that, according to the article, "certainly looked like lion tracks." One witness even claimed to have seen the lion eating a chicken beside the turnpike.

The inevitable big-game hunt for the Big Cabin lion occurred approximately during the third week of March, 1961. This may have been more of a threat than the actual lion. According to Tulsa zoo director Hugh Davis, "I'm not afraid of meeting the lion, it's those hunters. They're shooting everything in sight."

This may sound like just a fun story for the campfire, but what do the experts say? Both Davis and Roger County Sheriff Amos Ward think it likely. The best explanation could be that a lion may have escaped from a circus truck that overturned on the turnpike by Adair. Although there was no official report, area residents claim to remember the accident. It stands to reason if the circus people did lose a lion they may have kept it quiet to avoid any potential liability. Since 1961 no further evidence has been found to support the existence of any lion.

Most reports of cat-like creatures describe them as similar to black panthers. Although mountain lions reside in the state, their fur is reddish-brown to gray. Also, they are nocturnal, extremely secretive and only a few sightings have been documented. Even more rare than sighting a cougar in Oklahoma would be to sight a cougar with the melanistic recessive gene that would cause it to be all black. Having ruled out cougars, the identity of a mysterious black cat-like creature in Oklahoma is unknown.

Late one evening in 1956 such an animal was alleged to have been seen in El Reno. Jimmy Harmon was alone in a field harvesting wheat when he first saw the creature. Terrified, he ran home to tell his father, Melvin Harmon, who was quite skeptical about what the boy had seen. In an attempt to solve the mystery, father and son returned to the area, this time armed with a rifle at the younger Harmon's insistence. When the two returned to the field it was still there. The elder Harmon ran to the truck to retrieve his rifle, but when he returned, the creature had moved on, never to be seen again, at least in that field.

In 1969, a similar creature was again sighted in the area, this time nine miles north of Calumet. Howard Dreeson was driving on Ocharche Road when what appeared to be a black panther crossed in front of his car and disappeared into the brush.

In an interview with *Fate* magazine, Dreeson said, "It looked at me and its eyes shone. It was black as jet and had a real long tail. It must have been three feet long, maybe longer."

In Michael Wallis' book, *Way Down Yonder in the Indian Nation*, he mentions a creature named the Dog Creek Panther, in the chapter entitled "Oklahoma's Most Haunted." This tale takes place in Rogers County about ten miles northeast of Claremore in the small town of Foyil, Oklahoma. The creature got its name because for generations tales of a mysterious giant panther have come from an area known as Dog Creek.

The earliest known published account of the Dog Creek Panther was in January 11, 1908, in the *Foyil Statesman*. It reported that a local woman named Mary Tiger (an ironic last name) who lived a few miles outside of town, heard "strange noises" and "piercing screams" outside her home. Although an investigation found nothing, the newspaper reported a panther scare just east of Foyil later that same year.

According to Wallis there are still occasional reports of hideous screams and even panther sightings in the area. Two of the most interesting things about the Dog Creek Panther is, one, the creature is only heard and almost never seen, and two, the location. Foyil is approximately twenty miles southwest of Big Cabin, the home of the 1961 lion sightings. Is it possible that a thriving colony of large, unidentified, cat-like creatures could live in the wooded areas northeast of Tulsa without being recognized by the Department of Wildlife Conservation? It's hard to imagine any animal that cunning.

In some cases, witnesses give a description of something so unusual it's almost impossible to imagine. Early one evening in 1951, Mrs. Lawrence Laub of Calumet stepped outside to check on her cattle. When she reached the top of a hill between the farm house and the pasture she looked down to see a creature that as she put it, "looked like a cross between a wolf and a deer."

The creature was described as standing on four, thin deer-like legs with huge pads for feet. Its body and head were also described as deer-like, except that it was covered with long hair, had a bushy tail and pointed ears. It was bigger than a wolf or dog and the color of its fur was slightly lighter than that of a German shepherd dog's.

Mrs. Laub watched the beast for about half a minute, then threw a stick in its direction, the animal merely stared in her direction, apparently unafraid, motivating Mrs. Laub's swift return to the farmhouse. She kept looking over her shoulder to see what the beast was doing. She could see the creature just standing there staring at her until she was out of sight. When she told her husband about her encounter, he claimed he had seen a similar creature two years earlier. Mrs. Laub was quoted as saying, "There's a lot of underbrush out there and it would have been easy for it to prey on our cattle—but it never did. I really have no idea what it was. Some kind of freak of nature, I'd guess."

In late 1959 or early 1960, Ray Sutterfield was hunting in the woodlands near the east shore of Lake Texoma, ten miles west of Durant. While making his way through the bush he startled a creature which he watched jump several feet in the air, then leaped distances of "15 to 20 feet" until it disappeared into the woods.

Sutterfield described the beast as a cat-like creature with "pointed ears and a bushy tail." It was "dirty yellow" in color and had black stripes running along the side of its body starting at the shoulders. It had a body about four feet long and a tail about one and a half to two feet in length.

It appears Sutterfield may have stumbled upon an area known to be a hot bed for strange cat-like creatures, that is, if you believe the explanation a Texas woman told *The Paris News* in July, 1965.

Direct, Texas is a small town located approximately fifty miles southeast of where Sutterfield spotted his creature. A woman from Direct was quoted by *The Paris News* as saying, "We can expect in it the last part of June and again in October just before deer season begins. We figure it migrates through here yearly."

Direct residents call it "manimal" and claim its prints are so large a man can put both hands in one track. Its tracks indicate its weight to be about 190 to 200 pounds and look like a cat's paw, except unlike a cat, the claws are exposed. In June it travels to the west and in October it changes direction and moves eastward.

It allegedly runs in eight foot leaps and its cry is described as sounding absolutely blood-curdling. Try to imagine a bobcat cry which gradually deepens and ends up sounding like a man screaming in pain!

The following is an account of the "manimal" as told by an unnamed woman from Direct, Texas.

"One evening as I was walking around the house with a flashlight I turned at the corner of the house and must have startled the thing as much as it startled me. It made one tremendous jump and left the yard. I hurried back into the house and called my cousin. We stood at the window and watched it as it crossed a fence and then stood on its hindlegs staring back at us. It stood about six feet, two inches tall. Finally it walked away on all fours."

Not all stories of strange, unknown creatures occurred long ago. In 1982, in Cheyenne, Alex Inman and George

Mysterious Cats And Other Strange Four-Legged Creatures 85

Home of J. W. Jordan in the Cherokee Outlet, an area called the "Triangle," 1886.
Photo by William S. Prettyman, Arkansas City, KS.

Of all the game bagged by these early Oklahoma settlers,
they seem most proud of their bobcat.

Photo Courtesy of the Archives & Manuscripts Division of the Oklahoma Historical Society

Springer reported seeing an animal he could not identify walking on four legs. "It was bigger and broader than a dog would be. Its head pretty much sat down on its shoulders," Inman claimed. "It wasn't fuzzy or furry, but slick haired, like a pig. It was smooth moving. It didn't bounce any. It was pretty heavy, and had a pretty big body." Springer added. They reportedly honked their horn at the creature which it seemed to ignore as it ambled off into the brush.

So what can we conclude from all these stories? Are all the witnesses either lying or mistaken? It isn't impossible to imagine an exotic pet escaping from a careless owner. If only one of these stories is true, it would mean Oklahoma is home to an unknown species of big cat or something equally as unusual.

Howard Dreeson seemed to sum it up best when he told *Fate*, "Folks around here are always seeing funny things but they never like to talk about 'em. Everybody takes a sort of 'so what?' attitude. Just the other day a fella said to me, 'I seen something mighty strange out by the timber.' I asked him, 'Well, what was it?' and he said, 'Dadgummed if I know.' That kind of killed the conversation right there."

10 Bigfoot And Other Strange, Hairy Bipeds In The Sooner State

Its legend predates the arrival of the first white explorers. Reports of sightings have come from all fifty American states and all ten provinces of Canada. The Salish Indians of British Columbia call him Sasquatch, which means "wild man of the woods." By now you may have guessed I'm referring to the legend of Bigfoot!

My interest in Bigfoot peaked in the 1970's during my junior high years, when the movie, *The Legend of Boggy Creek* was popular. Advertised as a true story, the movie told of the Arkansas Foulk monster who was known to travel Boggy Creek, which flows from Arkansas into Oklahoma. The movie mentioned numerous times that the big shaggy creature "always travels the creeks!" The neighborhood where I grew up bordered what used to be a large wooded area, complete with a pond and a creek. It was there I would try to imagine what a Bigfoot encounter would be like, all the while clutching my trusty pellet rifle. As a child, it was fun to muse over such campfire legends. Now I need facts before I'll believe such a thing is real. I decided to familiarize myself with the history of the Bigfoot legend in North America. I learned the earliest recorded encounter between Bigfoot and white explorers occurred in 986 A.D., when Leif Ericson and his men first sailed to North America. The vikings returned home with tales of encounters with huge monsters, described as "horribly ugly, hairy, swarthy and with great black eyes." Elkanah Walker, a missionary to the Spokane Indians of Washington, wrote in a letter of a race of giants who live in the mountains. The letter read, "They hunt and do all their work at night...they frequently come in the night and steal their salmon from their nets and eat them raw. If the people are awake, they always know when they are near, by the strong smell, which is most intolerable." This account was published in *The Dairy, 1838-1848, of Elkane Walker*, by Clifford M. Drury. Even a United States President expressed his belief in the existence of such a creature. In his book, *The Wilderness Hunter*, published in 1893, Theodore Roosevelt recounted a tale of a large, two-legged wild beast, described as uttering a "harsh, grating, long-drawn moan, a peculiarly sinister sound." Roosevelt recounted a tale of two trappers whose camp had been repeatedly invaded by the strange beast. One trapper, named Bauman, returned to camp one evening to find his partner dead of a broken neck. The body of the victim had been thrashed around and "four great fang marks" were found in his neck. Bauman himself told his story to Roosevelt, who apparently believed him. In *The Wilderness Hunter*, Roosevelt wrote, "He must have believed what he said, for he could hardly repress a shudder at certain points of the tale..."

Throughout the history of North America, most Bigfoot-sightings have come from the area of the country known as the Pacific Northwest. Dr. Grover Krantz, visiting professor of anthropology at Oregon State University, has been researching the Bigfoot phenomenon for twenty years, and is convinced it does exist. Dr. Krantz told the *Tulsa Tribune*, "I'm satisfied that half the reports in my area are real." He also went on to say, "I don't have any real knowledge of the Oklahoma area...but the sightings in McCurtain County are similar to some reports from the mountainous, wooded states of Oregon and Washington." That's right folks. We got Bigfoot! Right here in River City!

According to an article in *Outdoor Oklahoma*, the state's first reported sighting occurred in 1849. Since then, sporadic sightings of strange, hairy, two-legged creatures have occurred in some of the states most remote regions. In 1926, two hunters reportedly caught a glimpse of a dark, hairy creature in a clearing near the Mountain Fork River. The men sicced their dogs on the beast, chasing it into the woods. The creature got away, but one of the dogs was later found ripped almost in two.

During the years 1974-75, a notable amount of sightings involving strange, hairy bipeds occurred in the Nowata/Noxie area of the state. These accounts received a lot of attention from newspapers, magazines and a couple of books on the Bigfoot phenomenon. One of the reasons for all the attention could have been the "Boggy Creek" movie, which was released about the same time. This period of activity began in late July, 1974, when Mrs. Margie Lee reportedly first saw the "monster" at the alarming distance of only six feet away. Mrs. Lee and her husband claimed to have seen the creature many times, when it would visit their property. "You wouldn't believe it," she said. "It could go as fast as or even faster than a deer."

The Lees and several other witnesses described the creature as six-foot tall, covered with inch long brown hair, and male. Mrs. Lee described the creatures eyes as looking "curious," so she concluded it meant no harm. She also mentioned a foul odor exuded from the creature.

Deputy Sheriffs Gilbert Gilmore and Buck Fields reportedly saw the creature in the headlights of their patrol car. The deputies opened fire on the beast who ran into the safety of the woods, apparently unharmed. About a year later, the small community of Noxie, just a few miles to the north of Nowata experienced a Bigfoot scare. Gerald Bullock claimed to have heard the creature's call about six months before catching a glimpse of it. "I still hear that noise, you know, right now. I heard it last night (October11, 1975) when I came home."

Some descriptions of the Noxie beast (or beasts as it turned out) surpassed mysterious, sounding downright supernatural. Several witnesses claimed to have seen its eyes glow red without light being present to cause reflection. Even more bizarre was its apparent imperviousness to gun fire. Marion Parret claimed he fired at the creature on three different occasions with a 30-30 rifle. Each time he was sure he hit the creature, but only once did it respond, by swatting its arm. Kenneth Tosh claimed to have the same problem trying to shoot down the monster. He and two friends opened up on it with two shotguns and a .22 rifle. "I didn't see how we could miss," he said, "but it didn't even holler. It just ran off." Tosh claimed several encounters with the Noxie monster. The most amazing tale involved his brother-in-law. "We heard one. Then about that time there was another one out behind us and they was callin' towards each other. That's when we knew that there

was two of them." According to Tosh, the two men saw the original creature whose eyes glowed red, then saw the second creature, whose fur was more of a grayish color and had glowing yellow eyes. The two creatures were about three hundred yards away from each other and seemed to be calling back and forth. Another claim of Tosh was a three-toed track he found measuring about eight inches across the toe and two inches across the heel. Just one more aspect of the story to stretch the limits of the imagination.

Reports of Bigfoot activity in Oklahoma are not confined to any one area, but do seem most prevalent in the southeast corner of the state. In 1989, a period of Bigfoot excitement existed in the deep woods of McCurtain County around the town of Idabel. McCurtain County Deputy Sheriff Kenny McKee acknowledged reports from "probably a half-dozen or more people" describing a creature like Bigfoot. McKee noted, "I don't know why they would lie about it, or want to start a rumor." Although McKee says he has never seen a Bigfoot in the fifty years he's lived in the area, he conceded, "Evidently, there is something down there, but I don't know what."

State Game Ranger Mike Virgin was skeptical about the monster sightings, having heard reports of strange beasts in the past that were unconfirmed. Virgin went on to explain how the woods in this area have been the site of Bigfoot stories "probably as long as people have been here."

According to Virgin, "The Indians, Choctaws, had stories about them."

"I'm in the woods all the time, and I haven't ever seen the track of one. I haven't ever seen one. Of course, that doesn't mean anything." Virgin concluded.

Others in the area are convinced of the existence of a large hairy beast lurking in the deep woods of McCurtain County. Joe Atwood, a timber cutter and long time coon hunter, claims not only to have seen the monster twice, but also to have heard its screams. "It's just a real shrill scream. It sounds like a siren that's off-key."

Atwood claims to have encountered the creature in 1984 and 1989 while coon hunting at night. From distances of fifty to seventy-five yards away, Atwood described seeing a "big animal, seven to eight feet tall...dark-colored, (and) heavy made," lumbering away from him. The sound of the creature convinced his coon dogs to retreat from the woods. "Whatever this is, they don't want nothing to do with it," Atwood said.

Idabel High School track coach Skippy Smith is another local resident who encountered a strange, hairy biped while hunting about a half mile into the woods. It was a June morning in 1989 when Smith heard something big and strong thrashing its way through the brush. Through the gaps in the leafy cover Smith claimed to have seen the hairy, reddish-brown legs of a creature apparently walking upright. "I got the heck out of there," Smith said. "And I haven't been back since." During the summer of 1990, residents around the town of Tahlequah in Cherokee County reported a strange hairy visitor. Eventually, the stories attracted the attention of the Associated Press. Under Sheriff Dan Garber said the creature was first sighted August 1, then again a week later, about three miles east of the first sighting. "I heard they had at least two calls last night (approximately August, 14)," said a sheriff's dispatcher, who wished to remain anonymous. "In the last month, there's probably been about four calls a week."

The woman who first sighted the creature estimated it to be ten feet tall and about four hundred pounds. Deputy Joe Weavel investigated the first couple of sightings and reported finding several footprints. "They were pretty good size," Weavel said. "I could stick both my feet side by side into the track."

Garber told about a woman and her little girl, who live in the area and claimed to have watched as the monster stood up and walked down a hill away from their house. "It has a lot of similarities to a bear, but what is unusual is that it's always, described as walking on its feet," Garber said. Weavel said the little girl claimed the creature had frizzy hair all over its body except its face.

District Chief of the Wildlife Department, Joe Adair, has had to field many questions about the monster. "I believe it's a bear, but I have nothing to base that on," Adair said. "I don't believe it's a Bigfoot." However, he agrees with Garber it is unusual for bears to walk on their hind legs for very long. According to Garber, Cherokee County is no stranger to Bigfoot. In the early seventies a creature was sighted that caused a "big ruckus."

In many cases dealing with sightings of unknown creatures the question is, are the witnesses seeing an unknown animal, or a known animal out of its natural habitat.

Now hold on to your hats for this next part folks. As incredible as it may sound, real live feral monkeys have been found living in parts of the United States. Although not native to North America, researchers claim to have discovered three official populations. Loren Coleman, a cryptozoologist and writer, investigated the mystery of the North American apes and published his findings in *Mysterious America* (Faber and Faber, copyright 1983). According to Coleman, a group of squirrel monkeys live near Coral Gables/Miami, Florida and a collection of about two hundred rhesus monkeys live along the Silver River near Ocala, Florida. Most recently, a band of baboons were sighted along the Trinity River in Texas. However, these monkeys are too small and don't fit the description of larger primates reported in the bottomlands of America.

Coleman researched accounts of what appear to be chimpanzees for the most part, meaning hairy, tailless and ape-like, and ranging in height from four to six feet. It is not unlikely a chimp could have escaped from a zoo or circus, but to adapt to an unfamiliar environment and live long enough to grow to four or six feet would be no easy task. Part of this adaption process seems to be the ability to walk upright and to swim, two things for which primates are not known. This inconsistancy could mean the apes have learned a new skill, or that the witnesses were mistaken. The sightings investigated by Coleman dated back as far as 1869 and usually involved states from the south to the heartland. One interesting place was Monkey Cave Hollow, located four miles northeast of Scottsville, Kentucky. It was named by early settlers because, according to folklore, it seemed to be inhabited by what pioneers described as some sort of monkey. Apes can also be found in Hoosier folklore, beginning in 1941 at Mt. Vernon, Illinois. Reverend Marsh Harpole was squirrel hunting along the Gum Creek bottom when he saw "a large animal that looked something like a baboon." It leaped from a tree and walked upright towards him until it got too close for comfort. That's when the Man of God hit the creature on the head the barrel of his gun, followed by a few warning shots to send it on its way. After that were more monkey sightings, and more strange tales about their ability to leap from 20 to 40 feet in a single bound. There were footprints found, strange howling noises, and finally an alleged death of a farm dog that inspired a number of hunting parties, but nothing was caught. By late 1942 the sightings ceased, but in 1973 the little town of Enfield, Illinois, less than forty miles southeast of Mt. Vernon would be visited by a similar creature.

There is much evidence to support the claim that feral monkeys do (or did) dwell among the bottomlands of North America. As you might have guessed, Oklahoma is not without its own monkey tales. Early one morning in December, 1970, an El Reno farmer discovered the door to his chicken coop had been torn from its hinges and several chickens missing. The culprit apparently moved on all fours, leaving strange foot prints. On the door was an unusual hand print that measured seven inches by five inches. The farmer contacted a game ranger who in turn contacted the director of the Oklahoma City Zoo, Larry Curtis. Curtis noted that the thumb was unusually crooked, as if deformed or injured. In an attempt to identify the creature, Curtis and several mammology experts took prints of various zoo animals, but none compared to the ones found in El Reno.

According to the Associated Press, Curtis said, "It appears that whatever made the prints was walking on all fours." The only conclusion Curtis could draw after months of investigation was that it must be "some kind of strange looking man."

One year earlier, similar tracks were found in the Canton/Oakwood area, about forty miles northwest of El Reno. In

January, 1969, Deward Whetstone made plaster casts of tracks he found measuring ten and a half inches long and four inches wide. The tracks, found in the soft, wet ground, showed a deep split between the first two toes. The creature, who apparently moved by putting pressure on the outside edges of its feet, seemed to be some type of primate. Whetstone told Jerome Clark of *Fate* magazine, "There were tracks all the way across the road. I followed them to where whatever made them jumped the fence. There have been a number of sightings of a strange animal in this area."

In November, 1968, Roger Boucher of Oakwood claimed to have seen a "gorilla-like" animal in his headlights. He was five miles north of Oakwood when he saw the creature running across the highway.

Howard Dreeson, of Moore, owns a saw mill in Calumet, just thirteen miles west of El Reno. He claims to have seen, on several occasions, a dark brown animal he believes to be a chimp.

It was 1967 when Dreeson claims to have first seen the chimp. Since then he has left bananas and oranges in the wooded area where the sightings occurred.

"They always disappear," Dreeson told a reporter for the *Oklahoma Journal.* "I'm going to try and catch him if he'll let me get close enough to get a net over him."

He claims the last time he saw the creature was in October, just two months before the El Reno chicken coop raid. When asked if the prints could have been caused by Dreeson's chimp, Curtis said it was possible.

No monkey sightings or strange footprints have been reported in the area since early 1971. A lot of people have just laughed the whole thing off as a hoax, but a local game ranger warned, "A lot of people are having a big laugh over this. They are referring to the 'thing' as the Abominable Chicken Man. But they'd cut out the wise cracks real quick if they saw some of those tracks around their homes."

I'm not suggesting that wild monkeys are the answer to the Oklahoma Bigfoot mystery, but in the El Reno, Calumet, and Oakwood sightings there does seem to be evidence to support this claim.

The classic description of a Bigfoot is; huge, covered with dark-brown hair, large black eyes and exuding a horrible smell. Its tracks have five toes and are shaped like a human foot, except that the front ball where the foot is hinged is moved back a few inches. Tales of glowing red and yellow eyes or three-toed tracks would be inconsistent with most Bigfoot reports. The best accounts of Bigfoot that are consistent with the legend, at least as far as I have found, usually come from the deeply wooded southeast corner of Oklahoma. Just in case you're wondering, I realize hoaxes do occur, and for that reason, many bigfoot tales I've collected are not included in this chapter. McCurtain County game warden Kenny Lawson has a theory for the source of some tales. "There used to be a lot of whiskey stills in these hills. I think people started telling wild stories about anything they could think of to keep people away from areas where they might find something they shouldn't." However, in some cases, the integrity of the witnesses and details of the encounter combine to create a mighty interesting story.

One explanation for Bigfoot sightings occurring in the Kiamichi mountains between 1942 to 1977 could be attributed to D.B. Benson. Drafted when he was eighteen, he returned home to Heavener after going AWOL. Believing he was facing execution, Benson fled to the mountains with nothing but a bundle of clothes, a pistol, some ammo and a knife. When his ammo ran out, he learned to kill small animals by throwing stones. When his clothes turned to rags and fell away, he fashioned a loin-cloth out of an old piece of denim. "I completely lost touch with humanity," Benson said. "I talked to the animals, even sang to the squirrels. Living in the outdoors I rarely got sick. When I did, I'd take to a cave for a few days until the illness cleared up. Fresh streams became my bath tub, and fine sand became my soap. Soon I learned how to catch fish bare-handed for food."

After many years in the mountains, Benson's loneliness and the fact that he was getting old became too much. In 1977, at the age of fifty-three, he returned to his parent's house and knocked on the door. His eighty-three-year-old father and ninety-year-old mother were no doubt astonished. Eighteen months later, Benson received an other than honorable discharge from the Army.

I doubt we've heard the last from our mysterious, hairy visitors. I'm sure, as the years roll by, we'll continue to hear reports from people who will see strange things when they go in the deep woods; but that's to be expected. When in the woods, shadows, shapes, sounds and smells take on a whole new meaning. Add that to the unlimited human imagination, and you have an equation that equals future reports of mysterious creatures. So, the next time you find yourself alone in the woods remember to look, listen and stay alert. If you're lucky, you may see a deer, bobcat, or even a bear. Or maybe, just maybe, you'll catch a glimpse of a legend.

11 "You Should Have Seen The One That Got Away!"

Oklahoma's many lakes and rivers are alive with tales of monstrous fish lurking in the deepest areas where they grow to enormous size. The story, as I was originally told, alleged a diver was inspecting a dam (which dam, no one seems to know). When he reached the bottom, to his horror, he glimpsed two gigantic eyes set a few feet apart, apparently on the head of a giant catfish! The terrified aquanaut scrambled to the surface, refusing to ever return. Of course, I was thirteen, and it was my first attempt to stand on skis. I always thought the story was to encourage me to stay up longer, so the boat wouldn't have to keep circling back to get me. I've since learned to slalom, however, the legend of the giant catfish remains the same. One reason this story is believed to be true is because, occasionally, anglers in Oklahoma have dragged ashore enormous specimens which would easily fit the criteria of a "monster."

In 1912, an alligator gar was pulled from Roebuck Lake in Choctaw County. It is believed to be the largest fish ever caught in Oklahoma. According to the state game warden's report to the Governor, the behemoth unofficially measured 7 feet, 10 inches in length and weighed 196 pounds. Officially, the state record (as of 1995) in the alligator gar

Claudie Clubb's record flathead catfish in 1977.

Photo Courtesy of Outdoor Oklahoma.

division was a specimen weighing 182 pounds, found in a net set in the Kiamichi River, in 1991. Although these records would be hard to break, there have been some honorable mentions.

One morning in 1977, Claudie Clubb was checking his trotline along Lake Wister when, to his amazement, he found he had snagged a creature with eyes that measured about a foot apart. The fearless sportsman jumped in the water and wrestled to shore what turned out to be a state record flathead catfish; five feet long, three feet around the middle and weighing in at 106 pounds! The state record catfish in the "all around" category goes to a blue which weighed in just a tad more than Mr. Clubb's flathead. A record was set in 1988 when Dan Grider wrestled from Lake Texoma a 118 pound blue cat he caught on his jugline.

Oklahoma is home to a species of fish that, believe it or not, is shaped just like the state. A good description of the paddlefish would be a large rectangular body with a long "panhandle" of a snout protruding from its face. This toothless, plankton-eating oddity has been known to grow to weights of over 100 pounds, however it is not a game fish. Because of their diet, they won't swallow a baited hook or lure. For this reason, paddlefish are caught by snagging or other accidental means. Records for this species were set twice in 1992. The rod and line record is 112 pounds, set by Gene Johnson, who pulled a monster from Grand Lake measuring 51 inches long (not counting the snout) and more than 40 inches around the middle. The unrestricted state record, also from Grand Lake, goes to Charles Ham, who found a 134-pounder caught on his trotline.

Enormous fish share their watery home with skiers, swimmers and other sportsmen, which leads to an inevitable question; are humans in any danger? In an article pertaining to giant fish in Oklahoma entitled "Monsters," Steve Wagner, editor of *Outdoor Oklahoma* magazine, referred to the state's aquatic residents as "quite harmless." In a 1985 article in *The Daily Oklahoman*, Kim Erickson, chief of fisheries of the Oklahoma Wildlife Department, was quoted as saying, "For a fish actually to bite someone in the water like they were going to try to eat them, I can't imagine that happening in Oklahoma." Erickson was responding to a claim by an eleven-year-old boy and his family, who saw him being attacked and pulled under the water by what was alleged to be one of the infamous giant catfish! Tommy Stanton was water-skiing with his family on Lake Eufala in an area known as Holiday Cove. The boy had taken a spill and was waiting for the boat to circle around for him when suddenly he felt something clamp onto his left leg! "It grabbed me and pulled me under the water twice. I couldn't think fast enough to know what to do," Tommy said. "I was scared." The family watched in horror as the boy screamed, "Daddy, he's got me! He's got me!" Michael Stanton courageously dove into the water and rescued his son. Tommy's left leg was bruised and scraped and had numerous puncture wounds, however, he wasn't deterred from returning to the water a few days later. "I guess I'm skeptical because I've never heard of anything like that happening. That doesn't mean it didn't happen," Erickson concluded.

Oklahoma is not home only to alligator gar, but real alligators have taken residency in state water ways. Primarily

196 lb. alligator gar. Fred S. Barde Collection.

Photo Courtesy of the Archives & Manuscripts Division of the Oklahoma Historical Society

found in the far southeast corner of the state, its range is sure to grow as the years roll by. According to the Department of Wildlife Conservation's, *A Field Guide To Reptiles of Oklahoma*, an adult Oklahoma alligator can range in length from six to sixteen feet.

If you're still trying to decide whether or nor to sell your jet-ski, here's one more story to consider. In 1981, a fisherman pulled an eleven-pound sand shark from the Arkansas River near the low-water dam at Sand Springs.

It would seem logical that the various creatures described in this chapter are examples of big fish, but certainly not the largest Oklahoma has to offer. I believe if someone wanted to break the state's monster fish record they need simply equip a large boat with deep-sea fishing gear and target the deepest areas of, say, Lake Texoma or Tenkiller. One thing for sure, most of these giants are bottom-feeders, responsible for keeping our lakes clean by eating rotting, organic matter that sinks to their depths. Having been assigned this important role in the balance of nature, it would be a shame if they were wiped out in the name of sport. As far as I'm concerned, just knowing they exist is good enough for me.

12 A Potpourri of Sooner Strangeness

The preceding chapters of this book have dealt with specific types of recurring phenomena involving significant numbers of Oklahomans. However, the realm of the unknown has no boundaries.

Most mysteries, such as UFOs and ghosts, are reported with such frequency that they usually fall into one category or another. Then there are cases I refer to as the "extreme" unknown; these would include events so unusual, they don't seem to fit into any category at all. Since there is usually not much to investigate, it would seem like all one can do is recount such tales and wonder. The only thing these remaining tales share in common is that they occurred in the state of Oklahoma. They can best be described as "random acts of strangeness."

Raining Toads in Beaver County

As incredible as it may sound, the phenomenon of the skies raining toads, fish, frogs and other organic material is known to exist. Charles Fort collected such tales that date back centuries. A potential explanation for a "toad fall" could be that a hard rain in some instances can cause toads to come up to the surface from under the ground. However, in the case of a genuine shower of organic material, roof tops and the tops of umbrellas become undeniably covered with whatever is falling. Oklahoma has a similar tale told to *Fate* magazine by a gentleman who drove a team of "broomtails" on a mail wagon in Beaver County, from 1908 to 1916. This particular tale took place sometime in late October, 1912, during "one unusually sultry evening." William W. Bathlot was about a mile from the Floris Post Office. He could see the black rain clouds filling the sky and noticed the heaviest, darkest area seemed to be directly overhead. A few minutes later, objects he took to be hail began pouring down on the mail wagon. Bathlot told *Fate* magazine, "In amazement I gazed at the thousands of small objects spraying outward and downward from the roof of the wagon and from the backs of my horses. They bounced up from the sandy soil like little rubber balls, lay stunned upon the ground for a few seconds and then flopped over on their stomachs as lively as you please. Among this myriad of small creatures I failed to see one killed or crippled from the fall. For some unknown reason they all landed upon their backs, thus protecting their little, soft, white bellies. I could peer outward for perhaps 100 feet through the falling rain and as far as I could see the top of the earth was alive with the little creatures. I held my hand out of the wagon window and caught four, fat, brown little toads all about the size of my thumbnail. Each was perfect, with legs and no tail. I had heard of fish and frogs falling from the clouds but I never had heard of a fall of toads. And these real honest-to-goodness baby toads were coming down upon the wagon top and upon the backs of my horses instead of coming upward out of the earth."

The toads fell for about three minutes but the rain continued in torrents. When Bathlot reached the post office, he found the shower of toads had fallen there too and just a little beyond. As close as anyone could tell, the toads fell in an area about a mile long and a quarter mile wide.

Another strange element Bathlot noted was that by October most toads should be almost full grown, whereas these were babies. Wherever the toads came from, it would seem they were out of sync with their regular growth cycle.

Phantom Blue Flames From Out Of Thin Air

The March 14, 1922, issue of *The New York Times* reported the story of a 23-year-old Alva woman who was apparently the focus of a fiery poltergeist. Mrs. Ona Smith, an invalid who lay paralyzed in bed, had to be accompanied by bedside watchers day and night who would put out the mysterious blue flames which would appear from nowhere and ignite various items in the room. According to the article, a new mattress burst into flames in the presence of several witnesses including a newspaper reporter. Bedding, clothes worn by Mrs. Smith, wall draperies and even a wall calender were only some of the items in Mrs. Smith's room to be reduced to smouldering ruins. Witnesses described the mysterious blue flames as giving off a "crackling" sound and seemingly jumping from the air.

A Mother's Curse

The death of Ponca City businessman Phinis (Jack) P. Ernest was officially attributed to asthma, but his doctor and his wife suggested that asthma was only part of the story. The man had been raised by a very domineering mother who helped him finance a nightclub, and then stayed on as a business partner. Fourteen years later, Phinis decided to sell the club, thus dissolving the mother-son partnership. His mother warned him that if he sold out, "something dire would happen." Within two days, he suffered a mild asthma attack, even though he had no history of respiratory problems.

Whether her prophecies about Phinis were psychic or self-fulfilling, they did seem to come true. For instance, she predicted his marriages to both his first and second wives would fail, and they did. On the other hand she told him his third marriage would be successful, and it was.

Phinis sold the night club. The next day he called his mother to inform her of the business transaction. "Something will strike you," his mother warned. His asthmatic condition immediately worsened and he was rushed to the hospital.

A psychiatrist helped Phinis see the connection between his mother's warnings and his illness. One day the doctor encouraged him to skip a scheduled visit with his mother. The result was a greatly improved respiratory condition. With his health on the mend, Phinis made plans for another business, one that did not require the assistance of his mother. He called to inform her of his intentions. She listened patiently, then warned he could expect "dire results" if he persisted. Phinis P. Ernest died in 1960, at the Veterans Administration Hospital in Oklahoma City, within an hour of his mother's prediction.

The Tulsa Kangaroo

An unidentified man walked into a Tulsa Cafe on Monday, August 31, 1981. He ordered coffee, then told the waitress he had just hit a kangaroo with his truck. He also told Tulsa Police Officers, patrolman Ed Compos and his partner Sgt. Lynn Jones. The individuals in the cafe were skeptical, until they looked in the back of the man's truck and saw a three and a half foot kangaroo. The man amazed the group further by revealing he had seen two kangaroos but swerved in time to avoid hitting both of them. The man finished his coffee and drove off down the road with the dead marsupial. Officer Ed Compos told reporters, "I wish I had taken a picture of it. I told the whole squad and they are laughing about it. There was a dead kangaroo! Everyone saw it."

Later in the same week, an Owasso family claimed they frequently had to dodge three-foot tall kangaroos while delivering newspapers early in the morning. About a month later on September 27, a seemingly related discovery was made when a twenty-five pound Patagonian cavy or mara (a giant long-legged rat for all practical purposes) was caught in Tulsa. The origins of the kangaroos and the cavy remain a mystery.

What Does It All Mean?

I believe people who find life boring must not be very observant. We live in a world full of wonder and amazement. I realize there are people so wrapped up in the "real world" that the topics discussed in this book would seem insignificant. However, sometimes these are the same people who find themselves in the middle of a mystery, with their lives changed forever.

It would be impossible for one book to encompass every

mystery involving the Sooner State. Mysteries continue to happen, and strange tales from long ago may never be told, unless the teller feels there exists an environment of acceptance without ridicule or judgement.

The 1990's hopefully mark the beginning of an era of greater open-mindedness concerning unexplained phenomena. Television programs such as *Unsolved Mysteries, Sightings, Encounters,* and *Arthur C. Clarke's Mysterious World* and *World of Strange Powers* have helped bring about an aire of acceptance to the mysterious and unusual. Indeed there exists in Heaven and on Earth greater things than are dreamt in "Horatio's philosophy."

As intelligent, highly evolved, thinking, biological entities in search of enlightenment we must remain open minded when confronted with new ideas. When Nicolaus Copernicus first expressed his belief that the Earth travels around the Sun and not vice versa, an enormous controversy ensued. In some cases individuals who attempted to promote this new idea were burned at the stake! An unwillingness to accept new ideas creates a breeding ground for fear and ignorance. As we move into the future as a people, it would seem likely that discoveries at least as significant as those of Copernicus will be encountered. Thomas Jefferson expressed the importance of an enlightened society when he wrote, "I know no safe depository of the ultimate powers of the society but the peoples themselves, and if we think them not enlightened enough to exercise control with a wholesome discretion, the remedy is *not* to take it from them, but to *inform* their discretion."

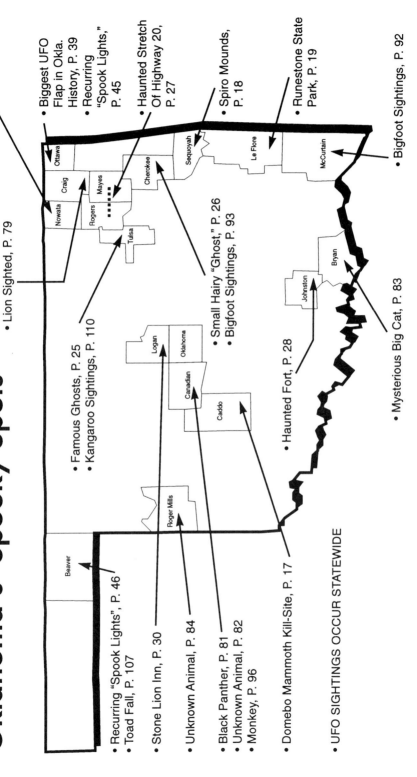

"Mysterious Oklahoma" References
(In order of appearance)

ANCIENT OKIES AND PREHISTORIC TOURISTS

Oklahoma: *A History of Five Centuries*, by Arrell Morgan Gibson University of Oklahoma Press (1981), p.9-13.

Oklahoma Treasures and Treasure Tales, by Steve Wilson, University of Oklahoma Press (1976), p.28-34.

Tulsa World, June 29, 1969, p.1, "State Stone Layer Forms Rocky Puzzle."

Edmond Booster, July 3, 1969, p.1 and 12, "Floor or Fluke, Formation Fosters Fuss for Finders."

Oklahoma Today, Summer 1973, p. 15, "Shu Shing Loa."

THE SPIRITS OF OKLAHOMA

Way Down Yonder in the Indian Nation, by Michael Wallis, published by St. Martin's Press (1993), p.198-202, 204.

"Oklahoma Haunts," produced by Randy Renner, (KWTV) Griffin Television, L.L.C. (1994).

Orbit Magazine, October 30, 1977, p.28, "When the Ghosts Walked."

Excerpt from *Unexplained Mysteries of the 20th Century*, by Janet and Colin Bord, (c) 1990. "Ghosts and Hauntings," p.86-87, "Ghostly Voices," p.187-188. Used with permission of Contempory Books, Inc., Chicago.

STRANGE SOONER SKIES

Oklahoma's Orbit, Sunday, April 18, 1965, p.6-7, "Flying Saucer Mystery Still Unsolved."

Copyright, 1987, Oklahoma Publishing Company. From the November 6, 1987, issue of *The Daily Oklahoman*, "Unexplained Lights Zoom Across Ponca City Skies."

Telephone interview with Hayden C. Hewes, April 18, 1995.

CLOSE ENCOUNTERS OVER OTTAWA

Associated Press report printed in the October 11, 1989, issue of *The Daily Oklahoman*, "Alien Tales Continue For Soviets."

Headline News, a service of CNN, Fall 1989.

Hard Copy, TV news magazine, Fall 1989.

Associated Press report printed in the October 11, 1989, issue of *The Daily Oklahoman*, "Baffling Lights Sighted."

Copyright, 1989, Oklahoma Publishing Company. From the October 13, 1989, issue of *The Daily Oklahoman*, "Mysterious Lights Make Encore Over Ottawa County."

Copyright, 1989, Oklahoma Publishing Company. From the October 14, 1989, issue of *The Daily Oklahoman*, "Miami Couple Injured in Car Wreck During Star Watch Party."

International UFO Reporter, Vol.3, No.7, July 1978, p.2-3.

THE MYSTERIOUS SOONER STATE "SPOOK LIGHTS"

Mysterious America, by Loren Coleman, published by Faber and Faber (1983), p.262.

Excerpt from *Unexplained Mysteries of the 20th Century*, by Janet and Colin Bord, (c) 1990. Used with permission of Contempory Books, Inc., Chicago. p.144-145.

News-Record (Miami, OK), October 30, 1992, "Tri-State Spooklight Legend Lives On," reprinted in the *UFO Newsclipping Service*, November 1992, #280, p.18-19.

CROP CIRCLES AND LANDING SITES IN THE "WAVIN' WHEAT"

Brandon Chase and Group One Film, "UFO'S ARE REAL"

Oklahoma Gazette, September 11, 1991, p.2-3, "Close Encounters of the Oklahoma Kind."

UFO Magazine, Vol.6, No. 5, 1991, p.17, "Unexplained Circles Found in Rye Fields in Oklahoma."

Copyright, 1991, Oklahoma Publishing Company. From the August 16, 1991, issue of *The Daily Oklahoman*, "Mystery Rings Prompt Telling of UFO Secret."

OKLAHOMANS AND ALIEN ABDUCTIONS

Oklahoma Gazette, September 11, 1991, p.3-4, "Close Encounters of the Oklahoma Kind."

Native Encounters, by Richard D. Seifried and Michael S. Carter. Copyright Seifried and Carter (1994). P.66-72.

Secret Life, by David M. Jacobs, Ph.D., published by Simon and Schuster (1993).

An Alien Harvest, by Linda Moulton Howe. Copyright Linda Moulton Howe (1989).

MYSTERIOUS MUTILATORS

Mysteries of the Unexplained, published by The Reader's Digest Association (1982), p.97-98, 101.

Copyright, 1992, Oklahoma Publishing Company. From the January 17, 1992, issue of *The Daily Oklahoman*, "Cow Killed, Satanist Tie Eyed."

Copyright, 1992, Oklahoma Publishing Company. From the January 22, 1992, issue of *The Daily Oklahoman*, "Police Link Mutilations to Satanism."

Copyright, 1992, Oklahoma Publishing Company. From the January 31, 1992, issue of *The Daily Oklahoman*, "Cattle Died Naturally, Tests Show."

Copyright, 1992, Oklahoma Publishing Company. From the September 6, 1992, issue of *The Daily Oklahoman*, "Lawmen Seek Cow-Maiming Cult Culprits."

Native Encounters, by Richard D. Seifried and Michael S. Carter. Copyright Seifried and Carter. P. 78-83.

Copyright, 1993, Oklahoma Publishing Company. From the April 21, 1993, issue of *The Daily Oklahoman*, "Mustang Police Ponder Mutilations of Cattle."

An Alien Harvest, by Linda Moulton Howe. Copyright Linda Moulton Howe (1989).

MYSTERIOUS CATS AND OTHER STRANGE FOUR-LEGGED CREATURES

Newsweek, March 27, 1961, p.31 and 34, "Lion at Large."

Oklahoma Furbearers, reprinted from *Outdoor Oklahoma Magazine*, published by the Department of Wildlife Conservation.

Fate, vol.24, 1971, p.64-67, "Manimals Make Tracks in Oklahoma."

Way Down Yonder in the Indian Nation, by Michael Wallis, published by St. Martin's Press (1993), p. 203.

Excerpt from *Unexplained Mysteries of the 20th Century*, by Janet and Colin Bord, (c) 1990. Used with permission of Contempory Books, Inc., Chicago. p. 242-243.

BIGFOOT, WILD MONKEYS AND OTHER STRANGE, HAIRY BIPEDS IN THE SOONER STATE

A+E's Ancient Mysteries, "Bigfoot."

Except from *The Wilderness Hunter*, by Theodore Roosevelt (1893), published in Reader's Digest's, *Mysteries of the Unexplained* (1982), p.152-154.

Tulsa Tribune, October 9, 1989, p.1 and 4A, "A Monster Mash."

Outdoor Oklahoma, March/April 1994, p.32-35, "Outdoor Myths and Legends."

Fate, vol.29, December 1976, p.70-73, "Oklahoma Monsters Come in Pairs."

Associated Press report printed in the August 15, 1990, issue of *The Daily Oklahoman*. "Bigfoot Rumors Fly in Cherokee County."

Mysterious America, by Loren Coleman, published by Faber and Faber (1983), chapter 15, "The North American Ape."

The Oklahoma Journal, February 28, 1971, p.1, "Hen House Terror Just Monkey Stuff."

Monsters, Giants and Little Men from Mars, by Daniel Cohen, published by Doubleday and Company Inc. (1975), p.123-125.

Fate, vol.24, September 1971, p.63-66, "Manimals Make Tracks in Oklahoma."

The World's Most Incredible Stories: The Best of Fortean Times, published by Avon Books (1992), p. 32, "Running from the Wars."

References

"YOU SHOULD HAVE SEEN THE ONE THAT GOT AWAY"

Outdoor Oklahoma, January/February 1995, p.9-11, "Monsters."

1995 Oklahoma Fishing Regulations, published by the Oklahoma Department of Wildlife Conservation, p.4, "Official Oklahoma Rod and Line Record Fish."

Associated Press report printed in the August 16, 1985, issue of *The Daily Oklahoman*. "Giant 'Catfish' Attacks Perkins Boy."

A POTPOURRI OF SOONER STRANGENESS

Fate, June 6, 1953, p.90-93, "Does it Rain Toads?"

Excerpt from *Unexplained Mysteries of the 20th Century*, by Janet and Colin Bord, (c) 1990. Used with permission of Contempory Books, Inc., Chicago. p.73-74.

Arthur C. Clarke's World of Strange Powers, "The Roots of Evil?"

Mysteries of the Unexplained, published by Reader's Digest Association Inc. (1982), p. 110. "A Mother's Curses."

Mysterious America, by Loren Coleman, published by Faber and Faber (1983), p.136.

To receive a copy of *Mysterious Oklahoma*, send
your name and address and $12.95, plus $2.50 shipping and handling to:
David A. Farris
P.O. Box 5991 • Edmond, OK 73083-5991
(Please do not send cash)